ECOLOGY AND SOCIALISM

Martin Ryle

RADIUS
An imprint of Century Hutchinson Ltd

An imprint of Century Hutchinson Ltd
62–65 Chandos Place, London WC2N 4NW

Century Hutchinson Australia Pty Ltd
P O Box 496, 16–22 Church Street, Hawthorn,
Victoria 3122, Australia

Century Hutchinson New Zealand Ltd
P O Box 40–086, Glenfield, Auckland 10
New Zealand

Century Hutchinson South Africa (Pty) Ltd
P O Box 337, Bergvlei 2012, South Africa

First published by Radius 1988

© Martin Ryle

British Library Cataloguing in Publication Data
Ryle, Martin
Ecology and socialism.
1. Europe. Ecology action groups
I. Title
333.95′16′0604
ISBN 0–09–182247–5

Printed and bound in Great Britain by
Mackays of Chatham PLC, Chatham, Kent

Contents

Preface

The relation between socialism and political ecology has been increasingly discussed of late. This book, a contribution to and extension of that discussion, pays especial attention to the British political context and to the perspectives and policies of the green movement and the Green Parties. I hope that, as well as continuing the red-green debate, it will play a constructive part in the building of an eco-socialist movement.

I am, of course, responsible for the book's arguments and conclusions; but in writing it, I have freely used others' knowledge and opinions. My first debt has been to the authors whose work is cited and quoted. I must also acknowledge the valuable journalistic work of *New Ground*, *Eco-News* and, especially, *Green Line*, whose unpaid editors, writers and production workers have both aided and chronicled the growth of green and eco-socialist politics. I would like to express my appreciation of the friendly solidarity I have enjoyed in working for and with the Green Party, in London and in Lewes.

Neil Belton at Radius offered editorial support and made valuable suggestions at various stages of work. I would like to thank Mary Kaldor and the United Nations University for commissioning from me, in 1985, a research paper some of whose conclusions are reflected in the present volume. Gerard Holden and Mary Kaldor invited me to help contribute an ecological perspective to a 1988 conference, and a collective book, on the 'new detente'.

Of the many people who have discussed socialism and ecology with me, I must particularly mention Roland Clarke and

PREFACE

Kate Soper. Kate, as ever, has given needed encouragement and loving companionship from first to last.

A note, finally, on a detail which may puzzle or annoy readers unless explained. I have used 'green' to denote the broader green movement, and 'Green' when referring to people or positions associated more specifically with the Green Parties.

Martin Ryle   *Rodmell, 1988*

1

Ecology Crisis
and Green Politics

The 'Limits to Growth' Reviewed

The ecology crisis is often thought of as a barrier, visible some distance ahead, to the continued expansion of industrial societies. It has been visible for at least a quarter of a century, as a huge body of literature attests; and its environmental symptoms are growing acute – the authors of the Brundtland report point out that during the brief period of their work, there were major disasters in Mexico City, at Bhopal, at Chernobyl and on the upper Rhine.[1] Still, the world's industrial economies continue to expand, though academics as well as polemicists assure us that the process must stop soon:

> If the present growth trends in world population, industrialisation, pollution, food production and resource depletion continue unchanged, the limits to growth on this planet will be reached sometime within the next one hundred years.[2]

> The old industrial system is at an end: the increase in material consumption and production, with the inbuilt waste, pollution and depletion of resources, has reached its *non plus ultra* and is enough to destroy us in a few generations.[3]

The Brundtland report (*Our Common Future*, 1987) comes as the latest authoritative study of 'present growth trends'. It enforces the familiar conclusion that 'hope for the future is conditional on decisive political action now'.[4] Anyone inclined to dismiss the green/ecological movement, whether from a techno-

1

cratic confidence in 'man's mastery over nature' or in the name of a militant socialism which dismisses the worries of 'middle-class eco-freaks', has to recognise that their arguments can carry no weight unless they engage with this literature and try to refute its prognoses.

Our Common Future highlights the systemic inter-relatedness of ecological crisis symptoms, and the interdependence of ecology and economy. Above all, it reflects its authors' constitution as a 'commission on environment *and development*': the pressure of industrialising humanity on the ecosystem is seen in the context of the unequal relations between developed and developing countries – relations whose injustice the text does not conceal. There is not space here for a summary of the report's conclusions, which would have in any case to be supplemented by a great deal of further data if I were trying to give a comprehensive overview of the ecology crisis.[5] However, both for the intrinsic importance of the material and because it introduces some of the political questions at issue, I will briefly discuss what *Our Common Future* says about the two key areas of energy and pollution.

Energy is at the centre of the debate about our ecological and industrial future. A huge fossil fuel 'energy subsidy' has made possible the industrial revolution in developed countries. According to one estimate, fossil fuels provided perhaps 7 per cent of the energy consumed in the USA in 1850, but a century later they 'contributed over 91% of total work energy and this percentage has further increased since then'.[6] Since these fuels form at infinitesimally slow rates relative to the pace of historical time, the energy subsidy is virtually a once-for-all gift. Yet it has habituated the rich countries to very high levels of energy consumption, both in industrial production and in domestic and private life. Moreover, continued energy abundance is assumed in certain technical responses to future resource shortage (for instance, metals reclamation). Are these habits and assumptions compatible with reality?

It is certainly true that, as the Commission notes, measures of conservation and efficiency have had an effect: 'in many industrial countries the primary energy required to produce a

2

unit of GDP has fallen by as much as a quarter or even a third'. However, 'by the early decades of the 21st century [such measures] will not alleviate the ultimate need for new energy supplies globally'.[7] While there are very large coal reserves and considerable quantities of natural gas – perhaps sufficient at present rates of use, though not of course under conditions of exponential growth, to last respectively for 3000 and 200 years – oil is in much shorter supply, with new discoveries unlikely to affect the conclusion that 'production will level off by the early decades of the next century and then gradually fall during a period of reduced supplies and higher prices'.[8] (Thus the Channel Tunnel, whose projectors vaunt it as the greatest civil engineering feat in history, runs the risk – dependent as it is on high levels of road traffic and of transportation generally – of being obsolete within a few decades of its completion.)

There are substitutes for petroleum (bio-fuels, coal-derived 'oil'), and there are renewable methods of electricity generation; though the Commission reached no consensus about the desirability of continuing with nuclear energy (some participants were from countries with considerable nuclear programmes), it stressed that in any case 'renewable energy . . . should form the foundation of the global energy structure during the 21st century'[9] – a foundation emphatically *not* being laid in the UK at present. But as the fossil fuel subsidy runs down, it remains uncertain whether present developed-nation levels of per capita energy consumption can be sustained *whatever* mix of options is chosen. No single 'energy future' is inscribed in the ecosystem, but all the various energy futures we might conceive of will have to observe resource constraints to which we have barely begun to accustom ourselves even in thought. This represents a great political and cultural challenge for the rich nations, even setting aside the pollution (see below) entailed by existing energy use.

However, only by broadening our perspective and thinking in global terms do we discern the true shape of the energy crisis. This is not just about environment/resource constraints waiting around the historical corner, but involves highly unequal consumption in the here and now (and there are of course great inequalities within industrialised countries: two cars in the drives of centrally-heated, five-bedroom houses; people suffering from cold and damp in one-room flats). Energy consumption in the 'Industrial Market Economies' is 7.01 KW years/year per capita, and the industrialised socialist countries are not far behind. In the 'Low Income Nations', it is 0.41 KW years/year (and this aggregated average obscures variations within the group: the level in sub-Saharan Africa is far lower).[10]

The first figure is 17 times higher than the second. This means that while we in the West soothe our eco-consciences by preferring lead-free petrol, and while our politicians of all parties weigh the electoral cost of putting a couple of pence on a gallon, people in the 'low income nations' spend ever longer stretches of their day gathering enough fuelwood to cook one meal. While we may worry about diminishing energy resources because the cost of flying might go up (big jets use a gallon of fuel every two seconds), people in southern Africa face the prospect that the trees which are their sole or main energy source, coming under unprecedented pressure of population increase and urban consumption patterns, will diminish to the point where there are just none left.[11] This is not, of course, a matter simply of the energy we use to heat our homes and cook our food and travel about: levels of energy use in industrialized countries reflect the 'needs' of industrial production, with its constant transformation of raw materials into (often rapidly disposable) commodities.

I am wary of invoking the poverty of the poor as evidence for a polemic. It is certainly true that a programme to improve living conditions in poor countries will require something more than a moderation of first-world appetites – and more than 'increased aid': it will require bilateral and multilateral economic action on a scale and of a kind which mainstream political parties have not as yet even contemplated.[12] But, at the very least, such a programme *will* require a moderation of (our) appetites. The authors of *Our Common Future* note that 'to bring developing countries' energy use up to the industrialised country levels by the year 2025 would require increasing present global energy use by a factor of five' – and this, as they go on to make clear, is inconceivable in terms of environmental consequences, even if the resources could be found and distributed.[13] They draw the inescapable conclusion: 'sustainable global development

4

requires that those who are more affluent adopt life-styles within the planet's ecological means – in their use of energy, for example'.[14]

Pollution is inextricably linked with energy consumption. Toxic chemicals from industry and agriculture, which enter the food chain or the water table or the upper atmosphere and escape 'beyond reach of cleaning',[15] are a serious threat, but the burning of fossil fuels raises the gravest problems both immediately and in the longer term. Today we already see increasing damage caused by acid deposition and we know that many cities and indeed whole regions suffer from dangerously polluted air.[16] The situation is particularly serious in central Europe: in the most heavily industrialized parts of Czechoslovakia, for instance, where

> smog is a constant and dangerous hazard. Life expectancy in northern Bohemia is between three and four years less than the rest of the country and infant mortality is 12% higher along with bronchial and skin diseases . . . Sulphur dioxide pollution alone is reckoned to have caused between £770m and £1.9bn worth of damage already . . . SZOPK [the independent Slovak Union for the Protection of the Environment and Countryside] report that pollutants like sulphur dioxide and nitrous oxide are already 13–15% above official limits and that the state oil refinery leaks 10,000 tons of unrefined oil into the Danube every year.[17]

Less evident and less predictable are longer-term and larger-scale effects, which may disrupt the eco-systems governing the world's climate. Industrial chemicals play a part here, but again it is the burning of fossil fuels, resulting in a build-up of CO_2 in the upper atmosphere and a consequent prospect of rising global temperatures, which is of prime importance:

> The 'greenhouse effect' may by early next century have increased average global temperatures enough to shift agricultural production areas, raise sea levels to flood coastal cities, and disrupt national economies. Other industrial gases threaten to deplete the planet's protective ozone shield to such an extent that the number

of human and animal cancers would rise sharply and the oceans' food chain would be disrupted.[18]

We may have heard this countless times but it cannot be over-stressed that the everyday functioning of contemporary industrial civilization is leading, at an uncertain but probably rapid pace, towards the point at which we will have damaged – perhaps irreversibly – not only the natural basis of human society, but the ecological balances on which the whole evolved life-system of our planet depends. It isn't surprising that the Brundtland commission, having outlined some necessary changes, declares:

> We are unanimous in our conviction that the security, well-being, and very survival of the planet depend on such changes, now.[19]

The limits of ecology as politics

I do not believe that anyone can read the extensive literature on the ecology crisis without concluding that its impact will oblige us to make changes in production and consumption of a kind, and on a scale, which will entail a break with the life-styles and expectations that have become habitual in industrialized countries. This general conclusion does not depend on predictions about particular depletion dates or environmentally destructive tendencies: Fritjof Capra and Charlene Spretnak are surely right to reject the optimism of those eco-revisionists who base their position on the inaccuracy of certain projections made in such studies as *The Limits to Growth*, and to argue that it is the un-controlled overall expansiveness of the economy that constitutes the problem:

> No amount of quibbling over the specific year in which we will deplete various minerals, ores and fossil fuels can alter the fact that we are living in a biosphere with a finite amount of physical resources. Pretending that the human race is somehow above the dynamics of the ecosystems, of which we are a part, is sheer hubris . . .[20]

Ecology, then, must enter as a limit, as a factor to be taken into account in any serious progressive politics. Since neither governments nor mainstream opposition parties are as yet prepared to come to grips with this limit, and in particular with its implications for economic strategy,[21] most of the political work of arguing for what Gro Harlem Brundtland calls 'changes in attitudes, in social values and aspirations' has fallen, as she notes, on 'people' and on 'non-governmental organisations'[22] – specifically, on the various single-issue movements making up the green movement, and on the Green Parties which, above all in Western Europe, have attempted to develop an ecological politics.

However, the mere invocation of 'ecology', crucial as it is, does not in itself determine in a positive sense the future development of social and economic reality. A society adapted to ecological constraints – and that adaptation might come about by the sheer impact of scarcity and environmental catastrophe, quite as well as by way of democratic debate and planning – could take widely varying forms. This is explicitly acknowledged by several writers, and is moreover implicit in the fact that very diverse 'sustainable societies' have been projected by different thinkers.[23]

One can imagine an authoritarian capitalist or post-capitalist society, with rigid and marked hierarchies of wealth and power, in which those at the top enjoyed ecologically profligate life-styles amidst 'unspoiled' surroundings, protected by armed police from the mass of the people, who would endure an impoverished and 'sustainable' material standard of living in dangerously polluted habitats: many lineaments of such a society were found in nineteenth-century industrial cities, exist on a world scale today, and are visible (both as actuality and as growing potentiality) even within modern first-world countries. One can imagine a 'barrack socialism' in which an ecologically well-informed, bureaucratic elite directed the economy in accordance with environmental and resource constraints, but in which the population participated as more or less reluctant helots, rather than as enfranchised and responsible citizens: tendencies in that direction might emerge in 'actually existing socialism' as the ecology crisis sharpens. Or perhaps the political and economic institutions of both market and state socialist

7

societies will prove incapable of mediating the pressures of unmet need and disappointed greed engendered by ecological scarcity (when, maybe, the 'period of reduced oil supplies and higher prices' sets in), and we shall have a kind of anarchy – not necessarily a pacific and libertarian kind. Tightening ecological limits will certainly affect relations between states, and the rich nations may well seek (are already seeking) to 'resolve' such a crisis 'independently of' – that is, at the continuing expense of – poorer countries. Some countries may retreat into autarkic self-preservation, others may seek closer ties of dependence on powerful allies; either way, as Raymond Williams has suggested, we are likely to see rising chauvinism and militarism and increasingly blatant armed intimidation.[24] The Rapid Deployment Force, US warships in the gulf alongside ships sent by the Western European Union: is not this in part a show of strength in defence of Western claims to 'our' oil?

A variety of visions, most of them dystopian, can be entertained, all of them feasible in ecological terms – and none of them particularly green. Ecological limits may limit political choices, but they do not determine them. The green movement may attempt to assess every option against ecological criteria, and may claim that all its proposals are compatible with sustainability; but we should not make the mistake of thinking that no other proposals, and no other outcomes, could be compatible. We should not assume that 'ecology' can satisfactorily define the new politics we are trying to develop.

Ecology: a 'new paradigm'?

'Ecology is not sufficient to define the new politics': there are some who would contest that claim by arguing that I use the term 'ecology' in too restrictive a sense. They would agree that what they would stigmatise as an 'environmentalist' approach does not engender an emancipatory politics, but would insist that the idea of ecology, properly understood, implies not just a critique of our environmental malpractices, but a positive guide to social and political regeneration.

A number of US writers (who, however, differ considerably

among themselves) have tried to show that 'ecology' can bear the weight of some such fuller meaning. They include those who have developed the notion of 'deep ecology'; those who advocate 'bioregionalism' and cultural/economic practices of 'reinhabitation' (Brian Tokar goes so far as to hail the bioregional idea as 'the conceptual basis for a full-fledged social-ecological transformation'); and those, like Fritjof Capra and Charlene Spretnak, who make large political and intellectual claims for the 'new paradigm' of ecology ('the first step in overcoming the crisis is to recognize a new "paradigm" – a new vision of reality').[25]

It is not easy to estimate the actual or probable influence of these ideas in the European and British green movement, with which the present essay is primarily concerned. Talk of 'new paradigms' has, at any rate, certain attractions for a political current which tends to insist on two related aspects of its self-proclaimed identity: its radical novelty, and its freedom from or transcendence of the left/right division.[26] If 'ecology' can do all that's claimed for it – if it can place us above and beyond all previous political struggle, if it is the sole key to a qualitatively different future – then 'the politics of ecology' may well be called, as Jonathon Porritt calls it, 'the only expression of genuine opposition to the dominant world order'.[27]

In my view, 'ecology' can't do all that.

Let me argue this at some length with reference to Murray Bookchin's ambitious work, *The Ecology of Freedom* – or rather, with reference to its opening and closing chapters, which set out respectively the conceptual claims of 'social ecology' and the utopian project which that concept is made to inform. One of the central tensions of Bookchin's argument surfaces at the outset of the final chapter, when he declares:

> After some ten millennia of a very ambiguous social evolution, we must re-enter natural evolution again . . .
>
> The history of 'civilization' has been a steady process of estrangement from nature . . . Today more than at any time in the past, we have lost sight of the *telos* that renders us an aspect of nature . . .[28]

9

Now our 'social evolution', surely, must be part of our 'natural evolution': if at some point humanity embarks on 'social evolution', this can only derive from our natural aptitudes as a species, and thus from the *telos* (the inherent and evolving meaning/purpose) of nature itself – if we want to posit a *telos* at all. The very 'estrangement from nature' of which Bookchin speaks (and of course he is by no means the first to use such terms, which are involved in the myth of Eden and the Fall) is our evolutionary destination. It is part of the *telos* that we should 'lose sight of the *telos*'.

In fact, the very phrase 'lose sight of the *telos*' is Janus-faced: cunningly ambiguous or usefully dialectical, as the case may be. It implies that there *is* a meaning inscribed in nature, but that we fail to see it. It has gone on existing, however, and we can now confirm its continued existence by 'catching sight of it' once more and so demonstrating that, 'ten millennia of . . . social evolution' notwithstanding, it was our destiny all along. On the basis of its reappropriated wisdom, we can 'make the implicit meanings in nature explicit' and 'act upon nature to enhance its inner striving towards greater variety'.[29]

Bookchin later writes at greater length about how we might 'enhance' nature. Here again he comes up against the paradox or contradiction: can human society be called 'unnatural'; how can it become 'natural'?

> We may reasonably question whether human society must be viewed as 'unnatural' when it cultivates food, pastures animals, removes trees and plants – in short, 'tampers' with an ecosystem . . . All of these seeming acts of 'defilement' may enhance nature's fecundity rather than diminish it. The word fecundity, here, is decisive – and we could add other terms, such as variety, wholeness, integration and even rationality. To render nature more fecund, varied, whole and integrated may well constitute the hidden desiderata of natural evolution.[30]

He goes on to suggest that human beings might become 'rational agents in this all-expansive natural trend'.[31]

This is the argument of Polixenes in *The Winter's Tale*: rebuked for suggesting that Perdita should grow 'carnations and streaked gillyvors' (products of cross-fertilization and thus created by the gardener's artifice), he replies:

> Yet nature is made better by no mean
> But nature makes that mean: so, over that art
> Which you say adds to nature, is an art
> That nature makes . . .
> This is an art
> Which does mend nature – change it rather – but
> The art itself is nature.[32]

Bookchin, like Polixenes, grasps the dialectical character of the relation of humanity and nature, and his book is no naive 'back to nature' manifesto. But although he doesn't advocate going back in time to a lost past, he does rely on the notion that we can find in 'nature', in its 'hidden desiderata', the values and meanings we need for our political project.

In my view, this is simplistic and misleading. Nature, like women and men, embodies contradictory tendencies ('Two such opposed kings encamp them still / In man as well as herbs – grace and rude will').[33] We can find in nature instances and images both of co-operative mutual aid (Kropotkin) and of Darwinian struggle for survival; both of expansive fecundity and of destructive violence. Human 'tampering' with nature often involves both aspects: we promote the 'fecundity' of our crops by killing the weeds in our fields. The eminently sustainable ecology of peasant farming has involved the regular slaughter of pigs and chickens.

Various theorists and ideologists have accordingly been able to find a variety of meanings in 'nature'. Bookchin himself, rejecting analogies from the natural world when these are invoked to support hierarchical ideas, is happy to turn to nature when it seems to confirm his own libertarian views: 'our closest evolutionary cousins, the great apes', he writes, 'tend to demolish these prejudices about hierarchy completely'.[34] He is well aware that authoritarian nature-ideologies can be, and have been, devised: citing E. A. Gutkind's phrase 'the goal of Social Ecology is wholeness', he admits that 'terms like wholeness, totality and even community have perilous nuances for a generation that has known fascism and other totalitarian

11

ideologies'. His response to these perils is to offer a definition of terms:

> a totalitarian concept of 'wholeness' stands sharply at odds with what ecologists denote by the term . . . ecological wholeness is . . . a dynamic *unity of diversity* . . .[35]

My own response is different. It is clear that terms like 'wholeness', 'ecology', 'the natural' are subject to various and contradictory interpretations and usages (hence, precisely, the impulse to define them). They are not unambiguous sources of political meaning, but sites of political disagreement. The political meanings attributed to 'social ecology' or 'the ecological paradigm' really derive from, and can only be discussed in terms of, traditions and debates (individualism versus collectivism, competition versus mutuality, authority and hierarchy versus liberty and equality) which long predate the emergence of ecology as a scientific discipline.

Green politics, then – the politics of the green movement and the Green Parties – is not simply any and every ecological politics: it is indeed 'imprecise . . . to use the terms "green politics" and "the politics of ecology" . . . more or less interchangeably',[36] for 'the politics of ecology' is itself an imprecise term. The values of the Greens, their commitment to justice and liberty, cannot be adequately anchored in 'ecology', but derive from a long tradition of progressive thought and struggle – liberal and libertarian and socialist.

The rise of the Greens in Western Europe

Since the founding conference of die Grünen[37] in 1979 (at which time precursors of today's Green Parties were already active in Britain and Switzerland), Green Parties have been formed in many Western European countries. As we shall see, they have won small but growing shares of the vote in local and national elections. This has been in part a 'protest vote' against the perceived failure of both governments and mainstream

12

opposition parties to develop policies in response to the ecology crisis. Beyond this, the Greens have become the focus of a broader movement of opposition/reconstruction, as the negative pole of ecological protest has attracted to itself a cluster of positive radical demands and visions. 'The future will be green or will not be at all': 'We are the alternative to the traditional parties . . . A radical reorganisation of our short-sighted economic rationality is essential': 'The politics of radical ecology embraces *every* dimension of human experience . . . the old age is giving way to the new . . . the turning point is already with us'[38] – the movement's spokespeople, it will be seen, like to characterize it not as a reforming environmental lobby, but as the herald of a new political dispensation. Many Greens, though not all, would explicitly connect what they see as the absolute newness of this political movement with its transcendence of the prevalent oppositions of established politics. Thus Jonathon Porritt hails the advent of die Grünen as marking the end of 'the redundant polemic of class warfare and the mythical immutability of a left/right divide'.[39]

Such proclamations of newness and transcendence cannot be maintained. The political development of the green movement must reveal the extent to which green politics draws (as I have argued it was bound to draw) on a common radical inheritance, and confronts structural economic obstacles and forces against which socialists also struggle. Nonetheless, the Greens *do* represent something new: a negative but essential recognition of ecological limits – and also, positively, one channel for the 'new social movements' (also courted by the Left) to find political expression and a new mode of political activism and activity which tries to avoid hierarchy and leader-fixation and is critically aware of processes as well as goals.[40] Nobody active on the Left, or engaged in radical politics, can neglect their advent.

By the summer of 1985, some nineteen green parties and electoral groupings were active in a dozen Western European countries. Representation at local, national or European level had been gained by Green Parties in Sweden, Ireland, Belgium, the Netherlands, Switzerland, Finland and Luxemburg, as well as, of course, in the Federal Republic of Germany.[41] The international reports published in the green movement press since then[42] indicate that the momentum has generally been maintained.

There have been some setbacks. In the UK, good results in the May 1987 district elections were not reflected in the general election which came shortly afterwards, where Green candidates averaged less than 1.4 per cent of the vote in the 133 constituencies they stood in.[43] In both France and Spain, political and personal rivalries have led to the formation of diverse parties each soliciting the green/ecological vote. In the Netherlands, the disbanding of the 'Green Progressive Accord' that had been organized (amidst some controversy) for the 1983 European elections, and the poor showing of the new Green party (de Groenen), presented the Dutch green movement with something of a crisis in the aftermath of the 1986 parliamentary elections.[44] *Os Verdes*, a Portuguese electoral grouping, was adjudged by a delegation from die Grünen to be 'an intentional set-up of the Communist Party'.[45]

However, the overall picture shows the European greens continuing to establish an electoral presence and gaining increasing support. In Austria, the newly formed Green Party won almost 5 per cent of the vote, gaining eight deputies, in their first national election (November 1987). In Switzerland the greens, who first achieved electoral representation as long ago as 1979, have developed increasing national contacts and co-ordination, though their primary organizational basis is still at the cantonal level; they now have some sixty parliamentarians, in nine of the country's twenty-three cantons.[46] In Sweden, where Miljöpartiet hosted the 1987 European Greens conference (in Stockholm in August), opinion polls in late 1987 suggested that a green vote in the order of 10 per cent was probable in the 1988 elections, which might give Miljöpartiet the balance of power.[47]

In Italy, the consolidation of a distinctive green electoral organization has been a gradual process. For some time, Luciana Castellina, a prominent 'red/green' parliamentarian, then of the small left party PDUP (though she has since rejoined the Italian Communist Party, PCI), sat with members of die Grünen in the Brussels 'Rainbow Fraction', a 'technical grouping' set up to distribute EEC funding among small radical and progressive parties. Both PDUP and the Partito Radicale, as well as the PCI, included environmental experts and publicists in their lists for the 1987 general election. By then, however, an independent green grouping had come into being, evolving from local and regional ecological concern and campaigning (for instance, a green group in the Marche won 3 per cent of the vote in the 1985 regional elections, before any national co-ordination existed). In September 1986, an international green convention was held in Pescara, and in the wake of this the *Federazione Nazionale per le Liste Verdi* was established, its candidates gaining 2.5 per cent of the vote in June 1987.[48]

Most crucially of all (since it is on the greens in West Germany that media attention and political commentary have mainly focused), die Grünen have established themselves as an enduring radical presence in the Bundestag and in State assemblies across the Federal Republic – with over 7 per cent of the vote, for instance, in traditionally conservative Bavaria. There have been intense ideological and tactical tensions and disagreements within the party, and the present disarray and imminent demise of die Grünen have been confidently proclaimed. Nonetheless, at the 1987 Bundestag elections they substantially increased their share of the vote and their number of seats: from 5.8 per cent (1983) to 8.3 per cent (1987), and from 28 seats (1983) to 44 seats (1987). It is with the confidence born of a now considerable political and electoral experience that Werner Hülsberg was able to claim in 1987 that 'the role of the Greens, in upholding a radical anti-capitalist alternative, will remain irreplaceable, whatever the final configuration of the Left may be in years to come'.[49]

Levels of popular support for the Greens remain quite low, of course (though we must recollect that these levels have been attained despite the fact that other opposition parties have presented themselves as the 'realistic alternative' to governments in office). However, the European dimension of the movement confirms its political importance. Co-ordination among the parties lessens the risks of any parochial and regressive 'localism': it is one thing to campaign against membership of the EEC and of NATO on a purely national basis, but another thing to oppose those institutions (as, for instance, the UK Green Party does[50]) in the name of a new internationalism. Regular dialogue and co-operation have strengthened shared ideological and strategic perspectives: the Western European green parties adopted a Common Programme for the 1984 European elections, and in 1986 they marked International Peace Year by jointly publishing a pamphlet (*From Two Blocs towards One World*) which set out a dealignment policy and included contributions from the UK, France, Denmark, Ireland, Belgium and the Federal Republic of Germany.[51]

It is above all in the Western European context that one perceives the Greens' challenge to the socialist, social democratic and communist parties which have, since the end of the nineteenth century, represented electoral opposition to capitalism and argued (with decreasing conviction, many would observe) for a non-capitalist alternative. Some of those who are turning to the Greens are moved by a sense that the opposition parties of the traditional Left no longer pursue, even at the level of rhetoric, any radically different conception of social and economic progress than is expressed by the avowedly capitalist parties. Green ideas have been gaining expression outside Western Europe, both in the states of existing socialism and in capitalist countries such as Japan, the USA, Australia and New Zealand:[52] but it is in Western Europe, with its long-established parliamentary tradition in which socialist ideas and parties have for many decades played an important role, that the red/green dialectic is most visibly being acted out.

2

Socialism in an Ecological Perspective

Several continental writers – Lucio Magri, Luciana Castellina, André Gorz, Rudolf Bahro, Erik Damman – have recently discussed ecological aspects of socialism, and although recent British books on the rethinking of socialism have often paid remarkably scant attention to environmental and ecological issues, there have been important exceptions, especially the work of Raymond Williams and Boris Frankel.[1] *Green Line* and *New Ground* have published a good deal of relevant discussion. Recent developments, on the British Left and in the UK Green Party, have opened up opportunities for red/green dialogue and co-operation, and it is possible that a distinctive eco-socialist political voice may be heard in Britain in the next few years.

I consider the tactical, organizational and party-political aspects of this prospect in my final chapter. Meanwhile,the development of eco-socialist ideas requires that both greens and socialists reconsider some fundamental assumptions, above all in the field of economics. It is certainly mistaken to think that 'ecology' can be enlisted, as a 'new social movement', behind the banner of labourism in the manner assumed by some Left writers:

> Although trade unions would play a central role, a number of other movements . . . would play an essential role in a socialist transformation. . . . The Women's Liberation Movement is the most important. . . . A socialist transformation . . . would not only involve all these groups but it would respect their autonomy and their expertise in certain fields.[2]

17

The weakness of such an approach lies in the assumption that the pertinence of new social movements is restricted to certain 'fields' (the writer specifies 'the family' as the relevant field for feminism). In fact, both feminism and political ecology question current and long-standing labour movement priorities in central economic and social objectives. The demands of new movements cannot be appended, as ancillary items, to the existing agenda, because they challenge important assumptions – the centrality of production and the marginality of unwaged labour; the commitment to economic expansion; the economic nationalism – which have always been central to that agenda.

One can of course respond to such criticisms by insisting that labourism itself is a betrayal of socialism.[3] One of the difficulties, in developing an ecological critique of socialism, is certainly to know quite how socialism should be defined. This haziness has allowed some green critics of socialism to attack it at one moment for its allegiance to social-democratic and neo-Keynesian economic methods, at another moment for its Marxist commitment to class politics. One need not share David Selbourne's bitterness about 'socialist illusion' to accept that he is justified in emphasising the heterogeneity of the demands and underlying philosophies that have been associated with the labour movement:

> Riven in a dozen different directions, [the Labour Party] contains those who are in essence reconciled to capitalism, and those who are not . . . For some, socialism is confined to . . . 'a broad human movement in defence of the bottom dog', and the defence of welfare; for others, it means a fundamental reordering of society and 'the comprehensive direction of the social process'. For some it is a 'commitment to production, liberty, care and peace'; to others, 'disarmament, devolution, abolition of the Lords and subsidized fares on the buses'.[4]

One can choose to simplify matters by dismissing as aberrations both Stalinism and social democracy, and defining one's own version of 'true socialism'. Conversely, one can follow Rudolf Bahro and dismiss all the unrealized promises and aspirations of socialists, confining oneself to the actual record and practice of self-styled socialist administrations and parties: 'Concepts', declares Bahro, 'are for doctoral dissertations. In reality socialism is what exists in eastern Europe, or it is the practice of the French Socialist Party, the British Labour Party, or Craxi.'[5]

I shall follow neither path, and will try to engage, in this chapter, not only with both social democracy and 'actually existing socialism', but with the socialist tradition of theory, critique and aspiration.

Social interests, ecological interests and the general interest

The fundamental tension between socialist and ecological perspectives lies in the fact that, while political ecology starts from the relation of humanity to nature, and with the general interest in ensuring that this relation is sustainable, socialism has concerned itself primarily with the distribution of power and wealth within societies, and specifically with the interests of a particular class, the working class, under capitalism. The socialist analysis of the relations of capitalist production discloses who benefits and who is oppressed, and envisages the ending of that oppression. The ecological critique, by contrast, focuses on the impact of a given level and pattern of material production on the eco-system: changes which affect only the internal relations between classes are irrelevant from this point of view. This disparity of perspectives can amount to a directly contradictory diagnosis, and give rise to opposed political and economic programmes, when – as has usually been the historical case – socialist parties and administrations have made the objective of higher overall productivity a key part of their project, and have regarded capitalist social relations as an obstacle to the achievement of a more rationally ordered *because more productive* economy.

I have argued that green politics cannot adopt a 'purely ecological' approach: relations between people and classes are at stake the moment one begins to talk about structural economic and social change, even if change is originally advocated because

19

of 'ecological' desires and fears. Moreover, as the green movement develops out of eco-protest and formulates comprehensive programmes, it finds itself asking not just what kinds of social relations are ecologically viable, but what kinds are good; and so confronts the questions about justice, autonomy and hierarchy, public and private spheres which have constituted political discourse since antiquity. It does so, what is more, in societies where many means and forces exist for the expression and mediation of social *interests*: trade unions, military-industrial lobbies, legal and financial institutions, elected assemblies, political parties . . . Ecological politics cannot fail to recognise that we are social/political animals as well as denizens of an organic biosphere. Its historical importance, and the tensions which it embodies and to which it gives rise in politics generally, derive from the 'double vision' which this dual realization entails.

Social interests can be and are expressed directly, by and on behalf of the groups and classes concerned. But the 'interests of ecology' can find political expression only through the activity of people – scientific experts, publicists, campaigners – who constitute themselves as representatives of those interests. (In the long run, and indeed already in the here and now, 'ecology', or rather its neglect and abuse, of course has direct effects of pollution or approaching scarcity; but a coherent, democratic response to ecological problems depends on our responding to them *before* they express themselves in these damaging ways.) Single-issue eco-protest campaigns, broader but still 'non-political' environmental pressure groups (Greenpeace, Friends of the Earth), and Green Parties represent successive stages in the attempt to give effective political voice to 'ecological interests'. They then tend to see themselves also as expressing a 'general interest' – the interest of nature, of a viable humanity/nature relationship – that is distinct from and even in opposition to the interests of each and every particular group/class within a social formation whose overall material reproduction is seen, rightly in my view, as unsustainable. 'I want to withdraw energy from the class conflict', says Bahro. 'Trade union activity is a retrograde step . . . this whole defensive struggle . . . guarantees the continued reproduction of the system.'[6] And Jonathon

Porritt dissents from 'the conventional socialist analysis of class politics' on the grounds that

> genuine redistribution of power can no longer be simplistically interpreted in terms of setting class against class, special interest against special interest: the need to serve the general interest of humanity now transcends any such old-world divisiveness.[7]

One response to this kind of green criticism is to accuse ecologists of ignoring the reality of class.[8] A more positive response is to argue that socialism itself precisely pursues, not just the 'special interest' of a particular class, but the general interest of us all. 'The proletarian movement' is said in the *Communist Manifesto* to be 'the movement of the immense majority, in the interests of the immense majority'.[9] In concrete contemporary terms, and philosophically too, the issue is certainly rather more complex than Marx and Engels allow here; but this is clearly the direction socialism must take if it is to respond to the ecology crisis and to the political challenge of the green movement. To redefine the 'general interest' so as to encompass the particular interests not just of the metropolitan working class, but of the poorest people everywhere, and to combine this with a serious appraisal of limiting 'ecological interests' – this certainly implies the abandonment of the labourist consensus around nationalist economic expansion. Such a radical redefinition, as I've argued elsewhere, could only be traumatic for the present Labour Party coalition.[10] On the other hand, a radical eco-socialism brings vital new arguments to the critique of capitalism, now seen as damaging to us all as well as exploitative of particular groups. It can also give new inspiration to what Barbara Taylor, in her feminist exploration of utopian socialism, calls 'a style of socialist endeavour which aims to transform the whole order of social life'.[11]

Utopian socialism

Utopian socialism would seem to be an obvious point of convergence between greens and socialists. Jonathon Porritt, despite the 'neither left nor right' position he has always

21

maintained, hails the 'inspired decentralism' of William Morris and laments the fact that it no longer guides the labour movement. Bahro admits 'if pushed, I would have to describe myself as a utopian socialist'. Robin Cook, the one prominent Labour Party politician to have written seriously on ecological issues and their economic implications, argues that a 'socialist ecology' would represent not so much a new departure for British socialism as a return to its native roots, and he too concludes that 'the future of socialism may lie more with William Morris than with Herbert Morrison'.[12]

Morris is the obvious point of reference in the British context. This novel *News from Nowhere* certainly fulfils the indispensable function of imaginative utopian thought in provoking us to question our own culture and society (for the essential negative features of capitalist industrialism which Morris identifies are clearly still with us), not just or mainly in critical polemic, but by imagining another society whose consensus about needs and whose sense of what counts as loss and what as gain run directly counter to our own. It also offers a quite detailed narrative of the politics of revolutionary change. This may be simplistic and has certainly proved too sanguine, since it envisaged a socialist popular uprising in the middle of the present century, but Morris has the advantage over many utopian theorists who virtually ignore even the political aspect of social transformation ('It is no accident', Ellen Meiksins Wood justifiably observes of the utopia projected in Gorz's *Farewell to the Working Class*, that Gorz's account 'begins with citizens waking up one morning and finding their world already transformed'[13]). Nor, of course, is there any need to underline the ecological aesthetic which attracts greens to Morris's vision of a frugal, gentle and non-exploitative social order based on harmonious relations with nature.

However, if we want to make something more of *News from Nowhere*, turning to it not as an inspiring vision but as the basis for a programme, then the difficulties emerge. Some of them are the consequences of Morris's own temperament and of the times he lived in: gender relations, for instance, remain obstinately pre-Raphaelite in tenor in his imaginary future. Others are more general, in the sense that they characterize

22

many 'escapes from history' imagined in the context of urban, industrial mass-production. There is the innocence about and tacit hostility to technology as such (Morris's sci-fi 'force barges' sound rather dubious in the nuclear era). There is the rejection of industry and the concomitant implication that all production can and should be the work of craftsmen and craftswomen in an essentially domestic setting. There is the overwhelmingly rural and agrarian character of the society.

As an assertion of values and an image of a distant future, this is quite legitimate and undeniably attractive. It corresponds to deeply rooted nostalgias, sorrows and fears – in literature, one thinks of Blake and Wordsworth, of Orwell's image of suburbia-as-dystopia in *Coming up for Air*, of old Alice Wilson in Elizabeth Gaskell's early industrial novel, *Mary Barton*, lost in idyllic visions of her country childhood as she lies dying in Manchester. (One of Morris's characters indeed refers casually to 'a place called Manchester, which has ceased to exist'.[14]) This imagining of the utopian future as in essence a transformed *past* (transformed, because purged of the oppressions and poverties, the ignorance and fanaticism, which as we know were integral to the actual past), this impulse to cancel not just the present but the long history which has given birth to it, reflects a cultural and psychological ambivalence about 'progress' to which green and eco-socialist ideas are partly a response.

Nonetheless it goes without saying that the response will be inadequate if it takes the form of an essentially regressive utopianism. That kind of vision is, first of all, fatally abstract in the actual midst of a densely populated, preponderantly urban society where almost all manufacture is by mass production. It is here that any eco-socialist changes have to begin. The regressive-utopian rejection of industrial production is also in my view wrong in principle, quite apart from its unfeasibility as the basis of a transitional economy, since modern factory methods represent immense savings in labour time, which might, in another society, free us for creative leisure. They give us, moreover, products (fridges, bicycles, kidney dialysis machines . . .) which few of us would willingly dispense with and which certainly cannot be made in domestic enterprises or craft workshops. We undoubtedly need a politics which reflects and develops widespread popular ambivalence about 'progress', but that politics has to go beyond the antitheses of rejection and acceptance, and articulate what Kate Soper has called a more 'compromised' response to modernity and its artefacts:

> These commodities are not without their uses, nor do we need to dispense with them altogether. The point, rather, is that they should be 'compromised'. We need to begin to pit their negative qualities against their more positive attributes, and thus little by little complicate a former more spontaneous urge to make use of them. As we watch the Nissan or Range Rover disappearing into a TV sunset at the desert's edge . . . we should recall that what these vehicles much more typically do is trap us in the din and stench of urban traffic jams, bring cuts in much less wasteful public transport . . . and depend on non-renewable oil supplies continuing to flow in from highly militarized and volatile areas of the globe.[15]

It would in fact be wrong to associate the green movement with any regressive utopianism, even if its traces are to be seen there – clearly in Bahro's incoherent 'commune perspective', more faintly but still unmistakably in the one-sided stress on 'the local economy' which characterizes green economic thinking.[16] Utopian imaginings, Arcadian as in Morris or high-tech as in Gorz, have their uses as well as their problems and contribute to the more complex and subtle work of devising political programmes and arguments. *News from Nowhere* is certainly an antidote to technocratic and productivist rhetoric such as has too often been associated with the Labour Party, and in that sense one can see that when Robin Cook cites Morris it is a step towards the greening of labour.

However, beyond these intellectual questionings and reservations, there is a further practical reason why 'utopian socialism' cannot be a viable meeting-place for socialists and ecologists. There are very few utopian socialists, many of them no doubt already in the Green Party, so an opening to utopian socialism hardly represents a real extension of the constituency addressed by ecological argument. What is needed is an engagement with the mainstream of the labour movement;

24

which means, in the terrain of ideas, with the assumptions of social democracy.

Social democracy and 'economic growth'

Socialism within Western Europe today means, overwhelmingly, the politics of the social democratic parties: the West German SPD, the British Labour Party, the French and Italian Socialist parties, and their counterparts. The ecological critique of socialism has thus focused primarily on social democracy, and in particular on the underlying commitment of these parties to economic expansion in the framework of 'managing capitalism': this will accordingly be the focus also of the present discussion. Before turning to that central theme, I must make a couple of introductory points.

The first concerns the commitment to 'bourgeois democracy' which distinguishes social democratic from Leninist parties. If I say that this is a commitment which I share, and which I believe to be widely shared too in the green movement,[17] I do not mean that I can conceive of no higher level of democratic control and popular accountability than is institutionalized in the particular forms of Western European political culture. On the contrary. Those forms can be criticized in the terms of the liberal-democratic tradition itself: we have encroaching 'official secrecy', imperfectly representative electoral mechanisms, opportunities (such as are afforded by the lack of any fixed term for parliaments) for governments in office to stage-manage general elections, growing remoteness of the executive from parliamentary control, subordination of parliament and the national executive to the secret decisions of bodies such as NATO's Nuclear Planning Group – which determined that 'we' wanted cruise missiles, and which, as I write, is about to inform us that 'we' also want to update 'our' post-INF nuclear inventory.[18] (In several of these respects, Britain is a less democratic country than are many of its EEC partners.)

Socialists would rightly take the argument further, insisting that however far we have democratized the political sphere, economic power continues to reside, as it must in a capitalist

25

economy, largely in the hands of unaccountable institutions. With all these reservations, however, it should be acknowledged that universal suffrage, a largely free press, freedom of expression and assembly, are all unequivocal historical gains. Their absence in most socialist countries has been a disaster both for the people of those countries and for the historical project of creting socialist democracy. An eco-socialist society, trying to institute political control of the economy, cannot draw its models of administration from the idea or the example of 'proletarian dictatorship'.

My second introductory point concerns the purely *environmental* failings of social democratic administrations and programmes. Within the framework of the economy as it is, there is scope for many legislative reforms to encourage and enforce better environmental practices: promotion of reclamation and recycling, prohibition of particularly polluting processes, outlawing of dangerous or dubiously safe pesticides, and so on. Although Labour local authorities, particularly the GLC, have done some valuable pioneering work here,[19] the Labour Party nationally has been slow to advocate such reforms (in the 1987 general election, the Alliance manifesto contained a fuller and more progressive section on environmental policy than did Labour's). However, this is certain to change, in response both to the promptings of the green movement – and particularly of the Socialist Environment and Resources Association (SERA), a Labour Party affiliate – and to the growing concern of the public at large. *Labour's Charter for the Environment*, and the summary of new Labour thinking published just before the 1987 election in the SERA journal *New Ground*, illustrate the beginnings of this change. While the Green Party predictably continues to take the lead here, green comments on purely environmental failings of social democracy are thus of secondary concern: I shall not be developing such comments here.

The fundamental green/eco-socialist criticism bears, not on the inadequacies of particular environmental policies, but on the overall economic orientation within which all policy is made.[20] While *Labour's Charter for the Environment* insists on something called 'sustainable growth' – that is, on the notion that 'environmental damage' can be limited even though 'our

26

economy must grow, new industries must be created, and old industries revived'[21] – there is little sign of the economic rethinking which such 'growth' (assuming that it were in truth feasible) would need to be based on. Even critics close to the Labour Party (SERA members writing in *New Ground*) insist that the interconnection between environment and economy needs to be considered much more seriously than it has been hitherto. Victor Anderson, for instance, comments as follows on the industrial strategy outlined in Labour's 1987 document *Industrial Strength for Britain*:

> [The document] *refers* to the environment (and a lot of other things) in one sentence but shows very little concern for the *purposes* of production, for 'socially-useful' production and for environmentally-responsible production. All it appears to be concerned about is *more* production and [it] effectively ignores the commitments made in the *Environmental Statement*.[22]

This undifferentiated commitment to '*more* production', which in part explains Labour's failure to take unequivocal positions on strategically important environmental issues (nuclear power is the most glaring example),[23] takes us from the discussion of environmentalism to the underlying question: the reliance of social democracy on the 'health', and thus the expansion, of the capitalist market economy.

The green critique of economic expansion has on the whole been conducted in fairly sweeping terms, with the result that 'ecologists', as Jonathon Porritt remarks, 'are always seen as the "no-growth party"', even though their actual position is more complex.[24] A sweeping and in a sense simplistic rejection of 'growth' is however an understandable response to an ideology, and an economy, in which expansion of production *in general* is the primary objective. The Left in and on the edges of the Labour Party has yet to mount an effective challenge to the rhetoric of growth: the Labour front bench has done nothing to develop a political language in which the questions of needs, of distribution, of the inadequacy of GNP as a measure of wealth,[25] of global inequality, of priorities between different kinds of

27

production, and also of ecological costs and limits, are brought into the discussion of economic futures, qualifying and countering the one-dimensional emphasis on producing *more*.

Indeed, the recession of the early 1980s led to an intensification of the traditional productivism of the labour movement, as the Conservatives' failure to maintain high levels of economic expansion became the main target of Labour Party attack. This attack was not conducted just by the front bench: left critics of Labour strategy, such as Andrew Glyn and John Harrison or the Labour Coordinating Committee, insisted in equally unconsidered terms on the need for 'faster growth'.[26] In 1981, Tony Benn could argue that a future Labour government would inherit 'a broken economy' and would thus be using public ownership 'as a way of getting public money into key areas of economic growth and development': the need for 'growth' was emphasised, but the 'key areas' were not specified.[27] The rhetorical keynote of Labour's 1987 manifesto remained the same: an advocacy of 'investment in industrial strength . . . a Britain with competitive, modern industries . . . modernising and strengthening the industries and services that earn Britain a living'.[28]

The eco-socialist response to all this has to distinguish between two ideological/educational tasks. First of all, the implicit assumption that 'growth is a good thing' – in itself, or in terms of human happiness – has to be made explicit and reconsidered. However, the argument cannot stop at that point: for underlying the social democratic advocacy of economic expansion is the fact that within a capitalist market framework, 'growth' is indeed the prerequisite of much else: especially, of the provision of welfare services and the creation of jobs, and of national economic status vis-à-vis other capitalist powers. Thus the critique of growth becomes a critique of capitalism and of the market.

Let us begin, however, with growth as such. In order to argue that a country such as Britain should in principle pursue expanded levels of overall production/consumption, a socialist would need to hold all the following beliefs: that the *average* per capita production/consumption of a contemporary Briton, which has more than doubled since the early 1950s,[29] remains too low to permit a good life (for of course the living standards

28

of the poor can be improved *without* the need for growth, by redistributive measures of the kind socialists advocate); that the desirable higher levels of production/consumption are possible for everyone, everywhere (for socialists surely cannot pursue wealth that depends on others' poverty, on continuing inequalities in resource use such as the Brundtland report identifies in the sphere of energy or such as André Gorz, drawing on the work of French development charities, catalogues in his essay 'Their Famine, Our Food'[30]); and that the expanded global production/consumption thus envisaged would prove indefinitely sustainable in environmental and resource terms. I suppose it is possible to hold all these beliefs: to maintain, for instance, that the energy use of a two-car family with five centrally-heated rooms is a model for the whole world population of the 21st century: but I doubt that they are in fact consciously held by many people. Rather, the notion of 'growth' has remained unexamined, even on the Left – just because to examine it is to confront the great historical facts of Western affluence, 'Third World' indigence, and impending ecological scarcity.

However, the green movement, especially but not solely in West Germany, is now beginning to dissolve the ideological and psychological barriers which have protected 'economic policy' from the impact of all these truly political questions about economics. A number of socialist thinkers have been responding to the ecological challenge and the new opening to a constructive utopianism which it is offering, and have considered the kinds of economic objectives that might develop as an alternative to an indiscriminate 'growth' whose effects, even in the rich countries which stand to 'benefit' from it, are in many respects destructive. Let me quote, as one example, this passage by the late Lucio Magri (E. P. Thompson has commented that Magri's 'definition of the matter is superb and I urge readers to return to it again and again'):

A pervasive crisis is now gripping the metropolitan societies themselves, in the common disarray of our industrialism, our welfare state, our parliamentary institutions, our primary social groups, our forms of conviviality. The problems of the Third and First World are in this sense inseparable from one another. For it

29

is not possible to confront the problem of underdevelopment seriously without putting into question our own ways of producing and consuming, our whole system of values. Any new relationship with the Third World presupposes a qualitative change in our own type of development . . . towards another style of development: one that was sober in its consumption . . . sought a reduction in labour-time performed, gave priority to improvements in the quality of living.[31]

The extent to which Labour, and the other Western European social democratic parties, prove capable of initiating and developing a more variegated and complex model of economic development, in place of the present simplistic advocacy of 'growth', will be the measure of the extent to which they are beginning to respond to the challenge of the ecology crisis and the green movement.

However, this will be possible only if and when the underlying commitment to the market as the final determinant of economic decisions is abandoned. I discuss the ecological deficiencies of the market, and the kinds of institutions that might begin to replace it, below.[32] Its basic flaw – its ineluctably expansive tendency – is evident, as was acknowledged by Robin Cook in his eco-socialist critique of Labour's 1984 Alternative Economic Strategy: 'as Marx recognised,' wrote Cook,

capitalism can only survive its contradictions by expansion and is incapable of aspiring to a steady state . . . The maximisation of profit demands constant gains in productivity, but without growth in output higher productivity results in higher unemployment leading to a recession in demand. Capitalism requires infinite growth which ultimately cannot be reconciled with a finite planet.[33]

A convincing 'alternative ecological strategy' would thus have to break with the social democratic project of 'managing capitalism'.

As well as qualifying the long-held expectation that the prime goal of economic policy is to ensure constantly rising levels of overall material consumption, such an alternative would have to find new, non-market-based means of providing employment and of meeting welfare needs, since in social democratic practice the market sector is not just an important source of jobs, but the tax base from which education, health, social security and so on are funded. An eco-socialist project also implies the very difficult task of breaking with the ideology of 'Britain will win' and establishing different patterns of trade with other countries. All these are questions which I discuss below.[34]

Class

Within the Labour Party and to its left, most of those who reject social democracy would declare their allegiance to a Marxist or near-Marxist politics, centred on the concepts of class and of socialism as the emancipation of the working class. The terms and meanings of a class politics of the 1980s are currently a matter of much debate among socialists. I cannot review this here, but it is part of the background to the present discussion,[35] whose focal question might be formulated in terms of the phrase quoted earlier from the *Communist Manifesto*: How far does the ecology crisis qualify or contradict the claim that the working-class movement represents 'the interests of the immense majority'?

Against the centrist rhetoric of a few greens ('. . . the redundant polemic of class warfare and the mythical immutability of a left/right divide . . .'),[36] and insofar as Green Parties have not directly challenged the structural inequalities of class and of the capitalist order, it is in order for socialists to make a few straightforward left-wing comments: to point out that we still live in a class society, in which the rich have lately been getting relatively richer; that democratic control over the economy, including the 'local control' on which greens argue new economic structures should be based,[37] involves a direct challenge to the power of the capitalist class (and in fact implies their disappearance as a class); and that 'if any green . . . alternative is ever to be implemented, it will depend on the support and participation of a majority of people – and especially of the organised labour movement'.[38] Having made these necessary points, however, socialists need to recognise that the question of particular and general interests, and of the capacity

31

of the organised workers' movement to represent the latter, is both vexed and crucial.

Raymond Williams put this at once forcefully and with subtlety in his contribution to *The Forward March of Labour Halted?*. Ecology is but one of the dimensions of his survey (though it is important that he, unlike other contributors to the volume, underlines 'the newly realized and decisive fact that we cannot *materially* go on in the old ways'[39]). He argues that when, historically, in 'the culture of poverty', workers organised to defend and promote their particular interests, 'the claim that these particular interests amounted to a general interest had a certain absolute cast. It could not be right for so many human beings to live like that.'[40] He then suggests how that claim is losing its 'absolute cast' when trade unions, within a rich modern society, continue above all to make their priority the defence of positions formed in and against the market:

> Other much more powerful interest groups, in the state, in the city, in the big corporations, are still there, combining, and the rest of us say: 'while they do it, we do it'. But they are not the only people beyond us. There are the millions of marginal and beyond-the-margin poor in our own country but also in far greater numbers in many very poor countries with which we trade. The indifference of modern capitalism to all those who live beyond the current bargaining terms and procedures is well known and shameful. But the question then is: do we join that indifference, or do we really try to surpass it?
>
> This is again the moment of socialism . . . It is the moment when we have to show . . . that our particular interests promote, are compatible with, or at least do not damage, the general interest. And then it is necesary to recognize that within the terms of ordinary bargaining – the everyday mechanisms of a capitalist labour market – this is only rarely certain to be the case.[41]

The argument has a readily comprehensible ecological aspect. There are, first of all, the 'interests' of workers in industries which any green economic plan would want to phase out rapidly. The nuclear industry, civil and military, is the obvious instance. 'I remember marching through Barrow,' a peace movement activist writes in *Green Line*, 'and realising that Trident was seen to be bringing work and hope, and life itself, to a jobless community.'[42] It is not exactly cheering to read, in the *Guardian*, of the unofficial blacklist at the Trawsfynydd power station, by which union members were advised which local shops had put up posters for an anti-nuclear meeting, and to note the comments of the shop steward who declared bluntly: 'People must realise that all anti-nuclear lobbying is endangering employment.'[43] Then there are manufactures such as the car industry whose products, while not directly perilous, would be of declining rather than expanding importance in an ecological economy. Finally and above all, there is the fact that an ecological economic strategy could not be based on the agglomeration, via 'growth', of particular interests into an expansionist pseudo-general interest. Reviewing *Labour's Charter for the Environment*, Victor Anderson and Jeff Cooper noted:

> Some unions have a very direct interest in environmentally-sound policies: e.g. in favour of the railways. Others don't – and this has resulted in, for example, the Labour Party publishing, shortly before the Environment Charter, and also as part of the Jobs and Industry Campaign, *Labour and the Motor Industry*, advocating the production of lots more cars, to fill Britain's sadly empty streets. This clearly reflects what the AUEW sees as the interests of its members.[44]

It is easy to feel that we are at an impasse.

This, then, is the difficult ground from which we start, and a proper appreciation of its difficulty is more helpful than abstract proclamations of the need for an alliance between the labour movement and the green movement. Yet that such an alliance will be necessary, that it must be the political objective of eco-socialists in green movement and labour movement alike, is hardly in doubt. Unless one envisages an authoritarian imposition of ecological wisdom from above, it is clear that workers have to be involved at every stage in formulating and implementing what Williams calls 'the concept of a practical and possible general interest, which really does include all reasonable particular interests' and which 'has to be negotiated, found, agreed, constructed'.[45]

'Negotiation' implies, first of all, that those who work in industries affected by ecological restructuring would have to be involved in developing alternative production. More generally, it implies an overall strategy – for employment, incomes and the distribution of wealth, welfare – which would ensure that workers were not exposed to the radical insecurity of capitalist restructuring, and which would envisage the removal of structural inequalities of class and the creation of a society of equals.

However, these economic objectives do not in themselves address the whole question. For this, we have to recognize that workers – all of us – have, not one 'particular interest', but *self-contradictory* interests. We want new cars, but we also want environments in which children can play safely, old people can cross the road unhurriedly, and we can hear each other talk in the street. Some of us may want 'success' for 'Britain', but many of us also find it intolerable to contemplate the gulf between our affluence and other people's absolute poverty. We want a reliable supply of energy, but more and more of us also want to halt the ecological damage done by low-level radiation, acid rain, the 'greenhouse effect'.

But the labour movement institutionally represents just one aspect of this contradiction. Trade unions, as Peter Tatchell put it in an interview for *Green Line*,

> are tied down to immediate short-term bread-and-butter interests. They tend to define workers' interests as confined to the workplace, whereas in fact people are not merely workers, they are also council tenants, they are also consumers . . . It may be in the short-term interests of trade unions to fight and save jobs on every single occasion, but they also need to recognise that some jobs may not be in working people's long-term interests . . .[46]

It is the 'immediate short-term' definition of 'interests' which is fed, via trade union representation on policy committees, into Labour Party programmes, leading almost inevitably to generalized commitments to 'growth' and 'full employment' which exclude ecological – and many social – dimensions.

This exclusion is something of which working people are

perfectly aware. Peter Tatchell, citing the example of the National Union of Seamen who 'sacrificed their jobs in order to prevent the dumping of nuclear waste in the North Atlantic', suggests that 'if more unions took on these issues as legitimate areas of trade union concern, we might see a re-popularisation of the trade union movement.'[47] Even from a purely electoral standpoint, the refusal to address these contradictions, and the continued adherence to a one-dimensional representation of 'workers' interests' centred on the workplace, may serve the labour movement ill. It is worth noting that among the Green Party's candidates for the 1988 European Elections in the UK was Sandra Leyland, 'a founder member of the Colne Valley Miners' Support Group during the strike of 1984–85'. As she explained to *Eco-News*, her

> growing awareness of Green issues was transformed in 1986. 'The Chernobyl disaster,' she says, 'shocked me into the realisation that concern for the environment should be central rather than peripheral to our political thinking.' She has since been an active member of the year-old Huddersfield Green Party.[48]

'Actually existing socialism': the Soviet bloc

The rigidities of Eastern European societies,[49] and of East-West relations, appear to be giving way to a period of great fluidity. Change within the Soviet bloc is marked by all the contradictions inherent in the notion of 'democratization from above', but we may now be approaching the point at which an irreversible momentum will have built up. East–West relations at 'official', inter-governmental level, which during the early Reagan years were alarmingly tense and confrontational, seem particularly cordial and relaxed.

The green movement is hardly in a position to influence these developments directly at present (though in Germany, where die Grünen have actively supported independent peace and ecology campaigners in the East, established conceptions of *Ostpolitik* may already be acquiring an explicitly ecological dimension).[50]

Ecologists and eco-socialists will however be hoping that green ideas and initiatives can inform the 'unofficial' or 'citizens'' dialogue between political activists, East and West, which has been conducted in and around the peace movement, and of which the *END Journal* has been both the forum and the record.[51] It seems likely that inter-governmental 'new detente' may be built around mutual affirmations of the virtues of technology, efficiency, and even of the market-place.[52] A critical 'detente from below' – likely to grow more important and more lively as and when citizens of the Soviet bloc gain new freedoms of communication and of travel – might develop a trans-bloc ecological critique of this model of progress, in whose terms a 'restructured' Soviet Union is pressing towards its long-held objective of 'catching up with the West'. It is here, in the interface between ecology and political economy, that dialogue may prove most interesting – and difficult.

Meanwhile, Western ecologists who feel that they have moved beyond protesting against environmental symptoms, and are trying to build political movements and alliances to press for structural ecological remedies, must not forget that what may seem 'narrow environmental concerns' are acutely felt in many parts of the Soviet bloc. Summing up the evidence, Mark Thompson writes that 'Czechoslovakia, Poland, the GDR and, to a lesser degree, Hungary have long been recognised as eco-logical disaster-areas . . . Environmental degradation endangers people's health on a scale and to an extent otherwise unknown outside the Third World.'[53] The Chernobyl accident has both intensified and broadened this public anxiety, and has also made environmental groups in Eastern Europe more sympathetic to the anti-nuclear preoccupations of Western peace and green activists (indeed, some Soviet bloc environmental groups modified previously favourable attitudes to nuclear power in its aftermath).[54] While Chernobyl 'forced a trans-bloc "establish-ment" consensus around the virtues of technocratism out into the open', it also – and as a corollary – 'allowed anti-nuclearism to emerge as the central plank of a trans-bloc ecological platform of opposition'.[55] Even if they remain for the time being limited to the domain of 'protest', we are likely to see closer links between environmental groups East and West, and issues of ecology will take their place alongside those of disarmament and civil liberties on the agenda of European peace movements.

As dialogue and solidarity develop, an ecologically informed citizens' detente will necessarily recapitulate the experience of the environmental/green movement in the pluralist West, moving from an agreed focus of protest into the more delicate area of proposing specific alternatives. Such movement forward is implicit, in truth, in 'protest' itself, or the latter risks becoming incoherent. If we are opposed to the air pollution caused by lignite-burning power stations, to the nuclear generation of electricity, and to the ecological havoc wrought by large-scale hydro projects such as the Nagymaros dam,[56] then we clearly have to think about 'alternative energy' – and perhaps about alternative expectations as to its abundant supply. Admittedly, the development of positive programmes for ecological/economic change must involve the movement in a certain loss of innocence, and mean that it forfeits the 'anti-political' stance which some Eastern European writers (Vačlav Havel, George Konrad) have discerned, and welcomed, in green politics.[57] But the underlying connection between ecology and political economy (likely, I suggested above, to be the point of creative tension in East/West dialogue) impels one to develop systemic and structural conceptions: all the more so in that we have to respond to *perestroika*.

In so far as greens contest the type of 'growth' pursued in Western Europe and elsewhere in the capitalist world, they can only caution against its adoption in the Soviet bloc: and I have already observed that both the objectives and some of the economic levers of the Gorbachev reform appear to envisage a 'Western-style' emphasis on expanded overall production. But even as greens warn of the perils of 'growth', and eco-socialists ask whether there are not virtues as well as dangers in the centralized planning and politically ordered economy of 'actually existing socialism', we must acknowledge the real economic, ecological and above all political benefits of *perestroika*.

Modernisation and reform may bring important environmental gains: in the replacement or renovation of outmoded and polluting technologies and infrastructural systems (the Polish electricity supply network, for instance, is notoriously wasteful and inefficient)[58] and in the development of energy- and resource-conserving processes. The provision of more varied and abundant consumer goods, one of the objectives of *perestroika* (and one in which market mechanisms are likely to play a particularly important role), is certain to be widely regarded as a great advance. Eco-activists need to be self-critical about bashing out denunciations of 'consumerism' on the latest thing in word-processors: 'satisfying the consumer', which in rich Western countries may seem no more than a euphemism for the promotion and marketing of unnecessary commodities, has a different meaning in societies where levels of personal consumption are far lower than they are in France or the UK.

Above all, the expansion of the market can be seen as *politically* progressive, even emancipatory, in societies where political and economic power both lie in the hands of a bureaucratic state. Here, the granting of powers of commercial and productive self-activity to private individuals or groups can appear as a welcome and long overdue opening into a more pluralist and democratic culture. Moreover, centralized planning, which eco-socialists in the West will regard as a means towards the assertion of social control over ecologically heedless production, is no guarantee in itself (quite apart from its historically attested political dangers) of ecological responsibility: a *merely* centralized administration, ignorant or careless of the environments over which it presides, is quite capable (just like the UKAEA or the Eurotunnel consortium) of inflicting grandiosely damaging projects, such as the Nagymaros dam, on unwilling local communities and fragile local eco-systems.[59]

It is against this background that we have to assess Bahro's former endorsement of 'centralized social planning' (Bahro nowadays holds a very different 'commune perspective'):

My positive evaluation of the non-capitalist base of the Eastern bloc rests on two fundamental points. First, the relations of command are much easier to establish than in the capitalist system. Secondly, and perhaps even more important, the problems facing our civilization require centralized social planning if they are to be solved, and this aspect must not be abandoned in the necessary changes in Eastern Europe. It is always possible to discuss whether the market has a role to play in satisfying the needs of the population, but the general proportions of the reproduction process must be planned.[60]

Formerly imprisoned as a dissenting social critic in the GDR, Bahro has been well aware – and so must we be – of the potential for Stalinist deformation inherent in 'centralized planning'. Nevertheless, I believe that he is right in his rejection of the market as the overall determinant of production. When one comes to think about how to replace the market (see the following two chapters), to ask what forms of social/political control and ownership can create an authentically democratic economy, and perhaps to ask also whether a non-expansive and non-capitalist market might not be invented and instituted – when, in short, one tries (intellectually, at first) to transcend the plan/market antithesis – then a sharing of experience between independent thinkers East and West becomes particularly valuable. Take, for instance, George Konrad's reflections on the role and possible forms of 'self-management':

> If economic decisions are not to be legitimated by capitalist ownership of property, then either the government must legitimise them or else the associated producers collectively. If it is the latter, then there arise the key questions for self-management: who decides in the name of the associated producers? An elected body or a person? Or is it possible to create a flexible legal and financial system, with social property at the disposal of individuals, which could serve as an economic formula for self-management?[61]

Greens would add that such a system must also serve (and this greatly complicates the question) to place the overall working of the economy under democratically agreed and scientifically validated ecological constraints.

These are questions, for the moment, rather than answers. But the questioning of two 'alternative' systems reaches the point where we face, together, the prospect that European societies may take a new shape (perhaps a new relation to the rest of the world, too) if and when the Cold War thaws. Neither actually existing socialism nor actually existing capitalism offers a way forward: 'obsolete communism',[62] certainly, but – eco-socialists will insist – obsolete market liberalism too.

3

Green Economics:
Some Eco-socialist
Observations

Green economic policies can be criticized by socialists on the obvious grounds that they say little specifically about capitalism, and do not propose distinctly socialist alternatives. This is on the whole true of the body of theory and argument on which the economic policy of the British Green Party has drawn, which is represented in the work of The Other Economic Summit (TOES) whose recently published volume, *The Living Economy*, will be frequently cited in the present chapter.[1] Socialists might object, too, that while green rhetoric often implies a wholesale rejection of the economic status quo,[2] few of the concrete policy proposals envisage basic structural change, tending rather to suggest piecemeal ecological or social reforms. There is no advocacy of changes in the ownership of large companies, for example; and although the 1987 Green Party manifesto carries a marginal note pointing out that '52% of the UK's land is owned by a mere 1% of the population', the policy on land tenure – the levying of Community Ground Rent – stops short of envisaging any expropriation of that rich 1 per cent.

As a socialist, I am of course in sympathy with this line of criticism. However, the social democratic parties have hardly been advancing a distinctively socialist critique of capitalism, either, of late. Indeed the Labour Party's most recent manifesto, *Britain Will Win*, can hardly be said to offer *any* kind of critique; and the 'new realism' now in the ascendant does not promise to offer much of an ideological challenge to the market economy.

41

Meanwhile Werner Hülsberg claims that during its seventeen-year dominance of successive coalition governments, the West German SPD 'presided . . . over an undeviatingly orthodox administration of West German capitalism, without the slightest pretension of deep-going reforms, let alone socialist objectives.'[3] Replacing market laws as the dominating imperative of production, dismantling hierarchies of wealth and power, bringing the direction of the economy as a whole under democratic political control: if this is what we mean by socialism, if these are objectives that we regard as integral to an adequate strategy for social-ecological change, then we must concede that – despite the persistence of minority Left currents inside and outside the social democratic parties – they have not been on the mainstream political agenda, and hence have not been part of most people's sense of the possible, for many years now.

The green movement, then, while it may be an anti-capitalist movement both in the logic of its criticisms of 'growth' and in the consciousness of many of its activists,[4] comes into being at a time when 'socialism', as a project of overall economic reconstruction, is barely on the agenda. Moreover, the greens' commitment to a localist, grass-roots strategy for change, their libertarian and decentralist orientation, are at odds with much socialist practice and ideology. While the focus on 'human scale' and the local economy is in some respects inadequate (as I argue below), it is nonetheless a historically and morally necessary response to the centralist ills, including the political tyrannies, of Marxism-Leninism-Stalinism.

Against this historical and contemporary background, eco-socialists cannot rest content with the invocation of socialist generalities, which will carry little conviction – either within the green movement, or in the presentation of ecological policies to the public at large. Our arguments must go beyond generalities, and show how a socialist formulation can strengthen both ecological and social dimensions of particular policies. At the same time, a more abstract critique is also needed, and it is with this that I start.

The green critique of 'economic theory' criticized

The TOES collection, *The Living Economy*, includes contributions from a variety of national and intellectual perspectives. Alongside general theoretical papers, there are accounts of practical struggles and initiatives: among self-employed women workers in India, for instance, in the Kenyan 'Green Belt' tree-planting movement, or in small businesses on the US west coast. If there is one overriding theme, it is that 'economics is at an impasse'. The book's introduction and opening pages emphasise that, since 'the very assumptions of conventional economics are now unsound', what is needed is 'the most wide-ranging criticism of conventional economics'.[5]

By 'economics', economic *theory* is here meant.[6] Many of the theoretical contributions demonstrate that existing theory cannot grasp the reality of human well-being. New 'economic indicators', or social indicators, are suggested, which would reflect that reality rather than describing the circulation of money.[7] (This approach is echoed in the Green Party's 1987 Manifesto, in the claim that 'a Green economy . . . *measures itself using meaningful indicators* like health, low crime rates, human fulfilment and ecological diversity.'[8]) The argument, within its limits, is apt:

> The social costs of a polluted environment, disrupted communities, disrupted family life, and eroded primary relationships may be the only part of GNP that is growing. We are so confused that we add these social costs (where monetary) into the GNP as if they were real, useful products. We have no idea whether we are going forward or backward, or how much of the GNP is social costs and how much of it is useful production that we intended.[9]

It is difficult to resist adding that much of what 'we' currently 'intend' hardly qualifies as 'useful production' anyway: I am thinking, of course, of the armaments which are becoming a major British export and on which much government revenue is spent internally.

What few, if any, of the contributors properly acknowledge, however, is that these 'false indicators' that are the basis of GNP (which aggregates monetary transactions and makes no distinction between 'useful' and useless, 'intended' or enforced) are also *real* indicators. They measure the economic activity, and use the criteria, which concern the profit-accumulating institutions (companies, banks) by which our economy is regulated. If – to use Marxist terms – they 'indicate' exchange value without reference to use value, this is precisely what makes them satisfactory indicators of a system in which production is not for use but for profit. 'Conventional economics' is not a mistaken theory/ideology; it is the institutionalized practice of a system with particular agents and beneficiaries. Socialists hardly need to be reminded of this, but any awareness of the *reality* of 'rules' is quite lacking in a passage such as this – which pursues a theme of concern to any ecological economics, namely the relation between the 'private sector' and such non-profitable activities as education and health care:

> Not only have the rules of economics come to be regarded as sacrosanct, determining rather than being determined by human activity, but a sub-set of rules, the rules of accountancy, have come to be regarded as of particular importance. Thus, increasingly, the particular measure of the money rate of return has come to be seen as . . . the true measure of the worthiness of human endeavour.
>   . . . As a consequence, those activities that can best be measured by price . . . that is, those activities normally regarded as private-sector activities, are favoured; whilst . . . convivial and caring activities are either disregarded or put into the category of subsidy.[10]

As things are, these 'rules of economics' *do in fact* determine the division between profitable and non-profitable activities, and ensure that the former are 'favoured'. In a capitalist economy, private profitable enterprise (plus whatever publicly-owned profitable enterprise may survive) is the ultimate source of money. The state siphons off part of the money circulating through profitable firms (via company taxes, and taxes, direct and indirect, on employees' pay) and allocates it to non-profitable activity: teaching, health care, administration. This may be – in my view, is – undesirable ecologically as well as socially,[11] for it makes the satisfaction of non-profitable needs dependent on the maintenance and expansion of production in general. If we want to change this undesirable state of affairs, we must go beyond a critique of 'the rules of economics' (or of 'accountancy') and seek to alter the organization of finance and production.

Similar observations can be made about the discussion of 'growth' in *The Living Economy*. Here too, what is said to be at fault is a set of ideas or assumptions:

> An economy that is growing at 3 per cent per annum *is thought to be* performing adequately, more growth is splendid, less growth is worrying, no growth or negative growth indicates widespread economic failure. *The assumption is* that growth is good and more is better.[12]

It is certainly the case, as I argued in chapter 3, that there has been a dearth of political discussion about the desirability of 'growth', and that even on the Left 'growth' has been repetitively advocated when what we clearly need is a more differentiated and complex debate about what kinds of economic development would promote social and ecological well-being. However it is also true, as I also indicated (and as Robin Cook acknowledges in the passage that I quoted), that mere undifferentiated 'growth' *is* functional to the working of a capitalist economy. Capital is advanced at interest, and can only be repaid if a surplus is realised. Shareholders expect dividends, and move their investments into sectors where these are biggest. Investment in new technology comes from the profits of growth. Labour displaced by the resulting automation will be reabsorbed only if new and expanded markets can be created in new branches of production. When the mechanisms of growth and accumulation falter, in recession or as a consequence of restructuring in established industries, then whole sectors of production and regional economies go to the wall. The 'assumption . . . that growth is good' is painfully confirmed by the real phenomena of unemployment and crisis.

To sum up: the critique of conventional economic ideas is salutary, but remains insufficient unless it is understood and clearly stated that the ideas are not only false (they don't constitute the only or the optimum basis on which economic life might be organized), but true (they reflect, because they institutionalize, the exigencies of capitalism). It follows that if we reject the ideas, we must be prepared to confront the institutions which embody and enforce them, and to invent the new institutions of a different, non-market economy. The green movement cannot evade this prospect, for even piecemeal eco-reforms tend, as I argue below, to run up in due course against the barriers of existing economic rationality and its agencies.

Markets and beyond

Although socialism is based on a questioning of market economics, markets have played and continue to play a role in socialist economic theory and practice. In the Soviet Union, the Gorbachevian reform, on which I commented briefly in chapter 3, includes a commitment to market incentives and implies a return to some of the ideas of the mid-1920s. In Britain, current thinking in the Labour Party leadership represents a frank acceptance of markets, and this draws on such theoretical work as Alec Nove's *Economics of Feasible Socialism*.[13] Without attempting to review this theoretical debate, I will concede that markets, as contrasted with planning, have one undeniable and one putative advantage. It is undeniable that the existence of a plurality of economic powers is a counterweight to the concentration in the state apparatus of political and administrative power (though of course market institutions, when they reach the scale of modern transnational companies, represent in themselves major and unaccountable centres of control which in turn surely require subordination to political authority) the historical experience of the Soviet bloc certainly enjoins caution in the advocacy of a unified, centralized economic plan.[14]

It is putatively the case that market mechanisms, especially in an age of rapid communications and sophisticated information gathering, are able to satisfy the vast range of consumer wants more efficiently and less wastefully than the apparently more rational *a priori* methods of 'the plan' – though the information/

46

communications/market research which are sophisticated tools of 'post-modern' private capital[15] might equally be deployed by non-market planning agencies. For these reasons, and also because any transition to socialism will begin, in the West, from an economy dominated by market institutions, it may be right to question the slogan 'abolition of the market' and to think instead in terms of the development of an economy in which markets continue to play a role.[16]

From an ecological point of view, however (and also in my opinion from the point of view of 'welfare'), it is clear that the regulation of the economy overall by market laws is undesirable. This is recognized by several US environmentalists/ecologists who are by no means socialists: many of the relevant arguments are brought together in William Ophuls' thoughtful study, *Ecology and the Politics of Scarcity*.[17]

Ophuls identifies the 'premise of abundance' underlying the notion of the 'invisible hand' by which, in the theory of Adam Smith and his successors, individuals pursuing their particular interests supposedly produce outcomes in the common interest of all.[18] He emphasizes the short-sightedness of pure market rationality, in which, because 'the economic value of the future is understated or "discounted"' vis-à-vis presently available returns on invested capital, 'critical ecological resources essential for future well-being even 30 years from now' cannot enter the calculations of a 'rational' entrepreneur.[19] He points out that the price mechanism in itself is insufficient to induce either producers or consumers to respond reasonably to impending ecological scarcity,[20] and that 'producers lack market incentives to respond alertly and appropriately to many of the problems' that such scarcity will create.[21] He insists on the 'structural' incentive towards higher and higher overall production which we have already noted: 'in a market economy – where the market is *the* economic tool, not just one among others – all the incentives of producers are toward growth and the wasteful use of resources'.[22] These arguments, summarized here, are developed in detail and with exemplification, and the overall conclusion is unequivocal:

In short, an unregulated market economy inevitably fosters

accelerated ecological degradation and resource depletion through ever higher levels of production and consumption. Indeed, given the cornucopian assumptions upon which a market system of economics is based, it could hardly be otherwise: both philosophically and practically, a market economy is incompatible with ecology.[23]

This conclusion powerfully complements the classic socialist case against the market, based on the criticisms that it depends on and reproduces inequalities of wealth and power and that it resists collective political control. This converging double critique, ecological and social/political, is fundamental to eco-socialism. We have already noted, however, that the social democratic form which currently dominates Western European socialist politics actually implies *acceptance* of the market. Is a similar acceptance general in the green movement?

Green economic policies (and this is more than can be said of those presented in recent Labour Party manifestoes) have been prefaced with general statements critical of the market. We have already quoted the manifesto of the West German Greens to the effect that 'a radical reorganisation of our short-sighted economic rationality is essential',[24] and the UK Green Party similarly declares that 'there is something very wrong with the economic system that we have inherited' and that 'real wealth is not stocks and shares and money in vaults'.[25]

In detailed policy, however, the Green manifesto follows a course analogous to the social-democratic strategy of 'managing capitalism'. A range of fiscal and legislative interventions is proposed, whose intent is to moderate ecologically damaging consequences of current production, but which stop short of developing a systematic critique of the market or of outlining alternative institutions or changes in ownership. For example, there are proposals for taxes on the use of resources; for 'Consumption Taxes to favour human skills, long-life goods, economical use of resources, and a small-scale economy'; and for tariffs, subsidies and taxes to overcome 'the present false economies of scale and centralisation' and encourage the development of diversified local economies.[26]

Such measures, in themselves, are imaginative and useful. The fact that they run counter to the existing practice of capitalist firms is no objection to them politically: indeed, as I suggest in chapter 5, reforming ecological legislation, within the framework of the market economy, would help to establish the legitimacy of an ecologically responsible administration and to enhance its acceptability as the guarantor of the long-term general interest as against the established particular interests of the market. Economically, however, such piecemeal reforms run up eventually against the dictates of profitability. 'Economies of scale and centralisation' are certainly not 'false' from the point of view of the transnational corporations which pursue them: transfer pricing, the concentration of information in the hands of management and the deskilling and fragmentation of the labour process, the freedom of capital to move production to countries and regions where wages are lower and trade union organization weaker – all this is within the historically acquired prerogative of modern capitalism. 'Long-life goods' are obviously preferable from the point of view of sensible resource use, but built-in obsolescence is preferable from the point of view of capitalist manufacture. If the introduction of consumption taxes were successful, say, in increasing by 50 per cent the average useful life of automobiles (which is quite feasible technically), this would have a disastrous impact on profits, and jobs, in the car industry.[27] In principle, of course – that is, in terms of human well-being – the manufacture of durable goods is preferable just because it requires less labour (as well as less resources). In practice, however, in an economy centred on profit, a decline in turnover leads to unemployment. Here is 'short-sighted economic rationality', blocking our way with its immediately practical effects.

So green reforms are vulnerable to the charge that they are unworkable, as indeed they are unless and until they are advocated within the overall framework of a different economic system – in which, to quote the US environmental economist Kenneth Boulding, 'the essential measure' of economic health 'is not production and consumption . . . but the nature, extent, quality and complexity of the total capital stock, including in this the state of . . . human minds and bodies'.[28] Such a conception, although 'utopian' in so far as there is not presently any political force capable even of putting it on the agenda, is plainly realistic, and necessary, in ecological terms. Its development is the chief political work of eco-socialists.[29]

The local economy and the state

A commitment to the regeneration of 'the local economy' is one of the keynotes of green economic thinking. Where this envisages no more than the enhancement of local productivity and prosperity, it is difficult to see how it coheres with an overall perspective of more modest consumption/production: participants in a thriving 'local economy' will not necessarily be eco-ascetics when they come to spend their money on goods (plane travel, central heating, hardwood furniture) from outside the 'locality'. However, there is an ecological and internationalist rationale for ideas of local self-sufficiency, even if their underlying ideological basis is in a somewhat unexamined and (as I suggested in chapter 2) utopian/regressive rejection of modernity.[30]

The ecological rationale is in part to do directly with resource consumption. Much trade entails obviously unnecessary transportation and use of energy: 'British butter being sold in France at the same time as French butter being sold in England is wasteful nonsense'; 'here in Bremerhaven we unload cars from Japan and load cars for America'[31] (I might add that I once met an Italian truck driver who made his living by loading up with Italian potatoes, driving to Brussels to sell them, and there loading up for the return journey with Belgian potatoes). Greens have argued, moreover, that delinking from world markets, accompanied by greater national and regional self-reliance and by new bilateral trading arrangements, is a necessary step in ending the exploitative unequal exchange involved in present north/south trade – a point to which I return in my discussion of internationalism in chapter 4. It is also held that a greater sense of control over and involvement in the immediate economic environment is a cultural precondition for the fostering of a greater sense of personal responsibility for 'the economy' overall, and for the creation in particular of strengthened ecological awareness and a more active sense of justice. A more decentralized economy would be more 'surveyable', as the German Greens have it,[32] and amenable to direct democratic management. This point is made in Guy Dauncey's paper on 'Local Economic Regeneration and Cooperation' in *The Living Economy*. Observing that proposals for a 'New International Economic Order' have hitherto led nowhere, Dauncey suggests that this may be because such an 'Order' is 'something "out there", something that puts the responsibility for saving the world into the hands of government finance ministers', and comments:

> Maybe in order for the new international economic order to become a reality, we have to take power into our own hands, and establish new local economic orders in the villages, towns and cities where we live, all over the world.[33]

Greater local economic autonomy and self-activity is not a sufficient condition for 'saving the world' (nor does Dauncey, who gives some interesting examples of relevant initiatives, think that it is): but I am prepared to think that it may be a necessary condition. I also regard it as a good in itself. A sense of the immediate benefit, to known other people, of one's work – such as is enjoyed by a schoolteacher or a general practitioner or a market gardener or a car repairer – is an important need/ pleasure now denied to many workers: in its absence, wages become the be-all and end-all of work. More integrated local economies would be one element in restoring such a sense.

All in all, the green strategy of promoting the local economy does have its ecological and eco-political logic. I am in principle sympathetic to it; it is nonetheless important to note both the difficulties of implementation and the limits in practice of such a strategy.

As I have suggested, capital often deliberately splits up and sub-divides the production process, not just to enhance profitability but precisely to deprive 'local' workers of power over their work. They may well be manufacturing components or sub-assemblies

51

which are useful only as part of larger wholes,[34] and in any case their products depend for distribution, promotion and marketing on large, often transnational, corporations. Guy Dauncey cites the example, in his home town of Totnes, of the attractively sited timber-yard by the River Dart, 'probably Totnes' biggest single employer', which does not even feature in the annual report of the company, BTR, to which it belongs.[35] Capitalist investment in 'the local economy', which is often (and understandably in present circumstances) keenly solicited, as a source of jobs, even by socialist local authorities, creates, not autonomy and diversity, but specialization and dependence. Vickers at Barrow, BNFL in Cumbria or at Dounreay, are ecologically painful and familiar examples. A recent instance, reported in *Eco-News*, is the planned establishment on South Humberside of a massive chicken 'farm', to be built by Unigate:

> Unigate are preparing to move into South Humberside with chicken farming on a scale that has not been seen in this country before. They already have planning permission for about 18 rearing 'units' . . . have begun building a processing plant (slaughter house) on one of Scunthorpe's Enterprise Zones (where they don't need planning permission) and intend to build a feed mill (where they will import grain from the Third World) on the Flixborough Enterprise Zone . . .
>
> The estimated cost . . . is £55 million. Of course, it isn't all their money: grants of 15% or £3000 per job 'created'; exemption from rates until 1993; 100% allowances for corporation tax and income tax; and also capital expenditure on buildings . . .[36]

Local authority powers, used here and in many other instances simply to reduce capital's infrastructural costs, can of course be used differently, to work towards the establishment of diverse and genuinely local economies. However, while the 'powers' local authorities now enjoy are sufficient to *help* capitalist investment, they are insufficient to interfere other than marginally with its priorities, let alone to establish alternative production on a scale to compete with the likes of Unigate. The powers enjoyed by the GLC were considerable by comparison with those available to most local authorities, and the GLC worked hard to establish a stronger and more socially responsible local economy, but the experience of GLC bodies such as the Greater London Enterprise Board and the Popular Planning Unit was in many ways frustrating. Above all, attempts to intervene in 'the politics of production' where companies remained in private ownership were constantly thwarted and evaded: this, writes Robin Murray, 'was the one great lesson' from GLEB's experience.[37] If we remember, finally, that even these limited powers of the GLC proved unacceptable to the government and its supporters, the conclusion is inescapable: the possibility of creating the kind of 'local economy' that greens advocate is conditional on action by central government, both to cede power to municipal and rural development agencies and also to wrest power from the institutions that currently wield it.

Co-ordinated strategic interventions from above are necessary, not only as a counterweight to the centralized power of large-scale capital, but because there can be no question of promoting a single model of 'the' local economy. There are, and can only be, many different local and regional economies. Their diversity follows in part from the distribution of natural resources: fisheries, forestry, vine-growing and dairy-farming and sheep-pasturing, hydro-electric power generation, mining and extractive industry, tourism, import-export handling – these activities, and others, are necessarily restricted to particular localities, and imply specialized local economies which must involve themselves in considerable trade with other places. Alongside these natural factors are historically created divisions, above all that between city and country, which can obviously change only slowly and which imply a high degree of specialization, trade and exchange. Unless one believes that the workings of the free market (which have after all played a large part in creating the present situation) will of themselves co-ordinate these heterogeneous 'local economies' in mutually enabling and enriching ways, one has to envisage political co-ordination of some kind: within a framework, eco-socialists would argue, not only of sustainability but of much greater equality between regions and localities. To make such co-ordination possible, and to establish that framework of priorities, must involve assemblies and institutions above the level of any particular 'locality'.

'Basic income', social income, and equality

Basic income schemes have been advocated from various points on the political spectrum. Milton Friedman is among their proponents, the UK House of Commons Treasury and Civil Service Committee recommended an investigation of their feasibility in a 1983 report, and the Social Credit and Distributivist movements of the 1920s explored analogous ideas. The UK Green Party declared in its 1987 manifesto that its basic income scheme lay 'at the heart of [its] proposals for reform'. Die Grünen have spoken, rather more vaguely, of the need for 'a social redistribution of generated values and income'.[38]

The Basic Income Scheme proposed by the UK Greens is readily summarized (there is an exposition of its basis in *The Living Economy*, which gives an account of its rationale).[39] Existing benefits (child benefit, social security, unemployment benefit and most others) would be abolished, and in their place everybody would receive an automatic, non-means-tested payment, with certain additional supplements for housing benefit and for those with special needs. Apart from its administrative simplicity, the scheme is said to have other advantages: in particular, it avoids penalizing those who currently lose benefit when they find work (the 'poverty trap'), since basic income is payable to all, in work or out.

However, it has some evident drawbacks and limitations. The two most prominent are these: it is unclear whether the proposed benefit would really suffice to support a decent standard of living, and the scheme does nothing to tackle low pay, which it might in fact encourage. The Green Party manifesto says that the scheme would 'guarantee an income adequate to live on, higher than current welfare benefits' and that 'all low income households' would have 'at least what they receive now'.[40] The TOES article cited figures (in 1985) of £28 per week per adult and £12 per week per child.[41] Paltry amounts like this are hardly consistent with the manifesto commitment to 'a taxation system that will radically redistribute wealth', to the radical egalitarianism that some greens profess, or to the requirement that, in a context of static or reduced consumption, basic economic security should be guaranteed to all.[42] that 'the Basic Income Scheme is not a charter for low-paid jobs', but we have been assured only a couple of sentences previously that 'low-paid jobs would be more worthwhile with the guarantee of the Basic Income; this would bring many more jobs onto the market'.[43] These faults, which in my view make the scheme, for all its prestige in green circles, useless even as a transitional tactic (we shall see that it is untenable as a long-term strategy), derive from the fact that the entire sphere of production and social labour is left untouched. Basic Income is a social democratic, purely fiscal measure. Exactly like the existing benefit system – which, trivialities apart, it replicates – it siphons off some part of the exchange value created in the economy and redistributes it by non-market mechanisms. If we need (as we do) 'a fresh approach to the way we organise work, the way we share it, and the ways in which people are rewarded for the work they do',[44] and if this is to open the way to progressive social and ecological objectives, then something different from the Basic Income Scheme is called for.

In considering what this might be, we need to ask what the ecological objectives of 'basic income' are. There is an implication that the introduction of such a scheme would somehow help combat or transform the 'growth economy', but it is not shown how or why this should happen (and in fact the second paper on basic income in the TOES volume, advocating 'universal share ownership', actually and evidently depends on continued *expansion* of the economy for decades to come).[45]

The ecological intention of 'basic income' begins, I take it, in the observation that individuals in market societies depend for their means of subsistence on the functioning of the (expansive) economy as a whole. 'Basic income' is supposed to free people from this dependence, or anyway mitigate it, by providing them with a guaranteed cash sum on whose basis they would find it practicable, as they do not now, to work shorter hours, to devote more time to 'convivial' social activity (including the direct, non-market production of some of their own means of life: growing food, caring communally for children and the sick, and so on), and to undertake some of the needed but presently unperformed, because unprofitable, work of caring for the environment ('repairing houses . . . looking after the land . . .'[46]). Moreover, since it is envisaged as a redistributive measure (though as we have seen the proposed scheme would not have major redistributive impact), 'basic income' might reduce social and psychological pressures towards 'conspicuous consumption' and the inexorable development of new needs/commodities.

Now it might seem that some of these desirable effects could in principle follow. Provided with a guaranteed cash sum, some of us might opt out, wholly or in part, from the world of 'jobs' – and those who have been forcibly excluded from it might be less anxious to enter. But, where would this cash handout come from? As I have observed, the Greens' scheme as it stands is a fiscal device, in which the profitable market sector – often called, in green argument, by the euphemism of 'the formal economy'[47] – would remain the source of all money: this would remain the case even if taxes were levied, no longer on pay and employment (via employers' national insurance contributions), but on raw materials, energy and so on.[48] Society is thus divided into a capital-intensive, high-technology market sector, controlled by capital and employing a labour aristocracy of technical and production workers, and a remaining population which appears, in this arrangement, to be parasitically dependent on that sector (just as health, social security, and public services generally can be presented as parasitic on 'the wealth-creating sector' today).[49] Ecologically, as a means to outflank or run down the 'formal economy', the scheme runs up against its own inherent contradiction: for if the 'formal economy' is the basis of guaranteed social income, it will have to continue to produce sufficient money for redistribution to the whole society, and cannot in fact contract or 'wither away' at all. In other words, the scheme is supposed to free individuals from dependence on formal economic activity, but in fact depends on the continuation of that activity, on which each individual also continues to depend.

A similar contradiction – the same one, seen from a slightly different viewpoint – is identified by André Gorz in his discussion of social income in *Paths to Paradise*. He does pay attention to ecological factors and to the need for a new and environmentally sustainable model of production/consumption, but his primary focus is on automation and on the crisis which this represents for a wage-based distribution of income. Discussing various suggested social income schemes, he comments that in many of them (and this applies to the scheme we have been discussing) 'the break with the law of value – and with productivist logic – is not explicit'.[50] The values to be distributed, in other words, are still calculated on the basis of the labour value embodied in the products of automated production, which in turn is calculated from those products' market prices. But, says Gorz, automated production creates values properly incommensurate with the individual labours of the workers involved: its productivity is derived from the technical and intellectual inheritance of the whole society:

> Guaranteed income thus cannot be based on the 'value' of labour . . . Its essential function is to distribute to everyone the wealth created by society's productive forces *as a whole* . . .[51]

The prospect of redistributing money from the automated sector (comparable to the greens' 'formal economy') to those who do not work in that sector is thus eventually wrecked on the inherent contradiction that,

> as labour time drops, per year and per lifetime, the sum of contributions and taxes needed to pay for non-work will outstrip the yield of direct wages. Finally, the payment for non-work time will exceed payment for work. And so it becomes impossible to argue that the former should be deducted from the latter. What is being undermined is really the premise of industrial capitalism itself.[52]

Gorz's own analysis needs qualification. It has been interestingly discussed by Boris Frankel, in *The Post-Industrial Utopians*. Also interesting is Cornelius Castoriadis' exploration, in *Crossroads in the Labyrinth*, of the themes of equality, needs, and distributive justice.[53] To read these debates is to recognize that the presentation of 'basic income' in the work of The Other

Economic Summit and in the UK Green Party's publications remains bounded by narrow conceptual horizons. And these correspond to a political horizon: to the reluctance to advocate direct social/political intervention in production and the market.

Within an essentially social democratic approach, there are better means available to work towards the objectives, social and ecological, of the basic income idea. Socially – in terms of redistribution – increased social security and unemployment pay, and low or zero rates of income tax on the first three or four thousand pounds of earned income, would do far more to ensure basic subsistence. Such redistribution would need to be funded by higher tax on high earnings. That is one of its strengths, if one is looking towards a society of equals. Ecologically – that is, in terms of allowing people to disengage from the 'formal economy' – there is obviously scope for legislation to grant individuals the legal right to cut their own working week (with a pro rata cut in pay), and to oblige more jobs to be made available to job-share arrangements.[54]

I would agree with anyone who said such changes would not suffice to create a more equal, less competitive and less consumerist society, or to free the economy as a whole from the tendencies of the market to expansion, waste, pursuit of profit rather than satisfaction of need. To achieve that, we do need a more ambitious programme: an eco-socialist programme.

4

Eco-Socialism

In the previous two chapters, I have been exploring the relation between political ecology and socialism, by way of a critical discussion first of aspects of the socialist tradition and then of green economic programmes. In the course of this discussion, outlines have been emerging of an eco-socialist politics. In the present chapter, I further explore some aspects of a positive strategy for eco-socialist transformation, and reflect on how an eco-socialist party or movement might argue for them.

This kind of writing always runs the risk of being overly abstract and programmatic, especially when it is not clear what social forces exist which might implement the programme, or indeed put it squarely on the political agenda. The relation between arguments and social forces is however, in my view, a dialectical one. Eco-socialist movement and eco-socialist argument come into being together and reinforce each other. As to the potential form of the movement, this is something I consider in my final chapter: I will say here only that, while (as follows both from what I have said about class politics and from my own commitment to pluralist democratic forms) I have no thought of a classical revolutionary strategy, I am aware that the eventual scope of what I propose goes beyond what might be instituted through the existing parliamentary forms of the British state. However, those existing forms, and the political activity which they permit – electoral and party-political interventions, campaigns, publication and argument – provide the context for the initiation and development of eco-socialism.

I have tried to moderate or control the temptations of programmatic abstraction by relating what I say to present debates, taking account both of positions held by greens and socialist environmentalists and of those aspects of more general political opinion on which eco-socialist argument can build. There can be no doubt that 'environmental issues' command greater media coverage and evoke more public concern today than they have ever done. Whatever the difficulties, intellectual and practical, of working towards it, an ecological transformation of modern societies is an idea whose time is coming.

The State and the environment

The green movement has a strong decentralist and libertarian orientation, and anti-statism is also found, though not of course universally, on the Left. Much of my own argument hitherto, and especially my criticisms of the green emphasis on 'the local economy', runs counter to this anti-statist current. Most eco-socialists, myself included, doubtless *prefer* to imagine a decentralized federation of autonomous communities, producers' collectives and the like, co-operating on the basis of freely entered mutual association. If one is honest, however, about the objectives which an ecologically enlightened society would set for itself, it is difficult to avoid concluding that the state, as the agent of the collective will, would have to take an active law-making and -enforcing role in imposing a range of environmental and resource constraints. More problematically, an eco-socialist transformation, which I regard as necessary if we are to transcend the contradiction between ecological imperatives and market 'laws', implies the necessity of replacing the current, highly centralized institutions of capitalist finance and production, and here the state must play an active role also.

I do not think that there are serious political objections or resistances to the notion that governments can and should enact and enforce laws to limit environmental damage. A number of such laws already exist, of course, and even governments of the libertarian right are quite likely to be legislating further in such matters. The present British Conservative administration may eventually be pressurised into doing something about acid deposition originating from British power stations. Chancellor

Kohl's government has taken steps to require automobile engines to be less polluting. Bans on open incineration at sea of toxic waste, controls on the use of chemical fertilisers where they risk polluting groundwater: these are the kinds of state-imposed restrictions, currently favoured by the Greens,[1] which many European governments may well enact over the coming decade.

The acceptability of this kind of legislation derives from the proposition that government can and should act as the protector of the general interest as against the particular interests of given industries or manufacturers. The many nineteenth-century laws passed to improve health and safety in mines and factories, and to limit the length of the working day, illustrate that the state has acted, with the support and at the behest of popular opinion, in a similar manner for over a century now – illustrate, what is more, the general point that the laws and rational motivations of the marketplace have proved incapable, since the Industrial Revolution, of containing the socially and environmentally destructive tendencies of large-scale production. Where there have been economic costs (increased costs of production passed on to consumers as higher prices), these have not outweighed the perceived advantages of the legislation. Today, surveys have indicated that most people would be prepared to pay the increased electricity charges needed to fund the retro-fitting of coal-burning power stations in order to reduce acid emissions.[2] Of course, an increase in prices weighs heaviest on those who are least well off: to socialists, a sharing among all consumers of 'ecological costs' would be more acceptable in a more equal society.[3]

Rather than echoing a glib and generalized anti-statism, an eco-socialist politics surely has to build on this historical foundation and these still existing sentiments. Environmental and resource issues are precisely of a kind where the establishment of a general, and long-term, interest is a reasonable and evidently necessary political project, and where there are cogent arguments for greater collective control over particular manufactures and kinds of consumption. Beyond the sphere of pollution, but still in relatively easily negotiable political territory, lies the realm of resource conservation. Here, there is

61

scope for legislation to enforce (and grant-aid) better insulation; to require longer guarantee periods for consumer durables and to ensure that spare parts are available for extended periods; to encourage the separation at source of domestic refuse and the recycling of much of it; to control the wasteful packaging of goods, and prohibit the selling of goods in non-returnable glass containers. Such policies, advocated by the Greens, would be part of the minimum programme of any even mildly green coalition.

More problematic, no doubt, is the question of the more intimately 'self-policing' aspect of governmental authority. A per capita restriction on domestic energy use, or at any rate a graded price structure (the reverse of the present system with its fixed quarterly charges) to penalize higher consumption; reduced legal maxima for cars' engine capacities; an element in petrol tax which went directly, perhaps via local authorities, to subsidize public transport; a ban on the import of tropical hardwoods – these are sound ecological policies, corresponding to a 'general good' which citizens might recognise, but they certainly infringe on the freedom to consume as we like. If a party/movement were advocating such policies, or if a goverment legislated to enforce them, would not familiar libertarian arguments against 'state interference' win new adherents?

This is not a foregone conclusion (though it is a reason, again, why greens should beware of endorsing and reinforcing anti-statist rhetoric). The speed limit and the drink-driving laws are contemporary examples of 'self-policing' where public opinion clearly favours the restriction of certain individual pleasures. The rationing of World War II constituted a very wide-ranging state intervention (which had a strong egalitarian aspect) in pursuit of an acknowledged collective interest. Of course this was not 'popular': people looked forward to its ending; but despite some evasion it was generally accepted, because its necessity was recognised. It is surely not inconceivable that certain limits on private consumption might be accepted as ecologically necessary.

The wartime analogy is admittedly questionable. Environmental and resource problems are no doubt felt to be of long-term importance, but there is hardly a consensus that they amount to an immediate threat justifying far-reaching restrictions. Moreover, if ecological scarcity does impact as sudden emergency, within an economy and a culture of unrestrained market forces such as is now being established in the UK, then there is every reason to fear an authoritarian-hierarchical social response; perhaps even a neo-fascist alliance of big capitalism and populist reaction, rather than the broadly egalitarian common acceptance of common restrictions that marked World War II. This prospect underlines the importance of beginning now to construct arguments and alliances which may help build an eventual democratic consensus around the idea of ecological restructuring.

Ecological restructuring

The very idea of 'restructuring', as opposed to environmental protection through piecemeal legislation, invokes notions of planning, of political control of the economy, which have been driven into ideological retreat. The Labour Party, in its policy review conducted in the first part of 1988, seems keen to distance itself from what the front bench clearly see as an outmoded and electorally damaging hostility to the market economy: an editorialist in *The Independent*, ready as good social democrats always have been to proffer advice to the Left, suggests that Mr Kinnock might think of mounting a British Bad Godesberg, so as to 'draw a clean line under the party's Marxist Past'.[4]

Furthermore, an ecological restructuring cannot be presented as a straightforward improvement in living conditions. After some decades of an almost uninterrupted rise in material living standards, from which almost all employed workers have enjoyed some benefit, it has to be argued that 'progress' can no longer be defined in those terms. Citizens in a sustainable economy will have to reassess inherited and unquestioned expectations, for they

> probably cannot be allowed to use private property as capital, except in the most restricted fashion, or to treat land and other

basic resources as commodities divorced from their critical ecological and environmental role. So, certain kinds of rights that we now enjoy will indeed have to be given up. . . .

In sum, in the frugal state we shall not be able to retain access to all the appurtenances of our current 'energy-slave' economy; we shall have to choose carefully and wisely where to spend our limited resources . . .; some luxuries may be possible, but not mass luxury or all the luxuries we want.[5]

This clearly has to be a central theme of a serious ecological politics. It has indubitably socialist aspects: it involves a recognition of the common good which must curb individualistic wants, and it surely also implies a more equal and less economically competitive society – 'we need a breakthrough to greater social justice and security simply to make way for those fundamental changes without which there will be no future at all'.[6] Above all, it calls into being a collective subject, a 'we', able to make political and cultural decisions directly, and this implies the transcendence of the atomised individualism of the market-place as ultimate arbiter.

But despite these elements of socialist analysis and values, the notion of an ecological restructuring represents in many respects a break with, even an inversion of, the current Left and labour movement rationale for state intervention in the economy. An ecological socialism certainly does not adopt the classical view that the capitalist market is to be rejected because it inhibits the development of overall productivity: eco-socialist relations of production would not aim to achieve higher production, but to make possible a new and different structure of needs and consumption. The objective of 'full employment' would need to be radically redefined in a sustainable economy, and that of 'growth' would give way to the more complex notion of *development*.

In general – and this may become in time the principal political strength of an eco-socialist argument, even if in the present climate it appears a near-fatal liability – the aims of eco-transformation would not be presented as amounting to a better (more efficient, or indeed more equitable) version of existing economic practice, but as constituting a clear break: and only such a break, it can then be argued, will prove capable of dealing with the ecological crisis of which we are all at some level aware, but with which the market, and those political programmes which seek to expand its workings, are proving unable to grapple. Alongside an insistent stress on ecology and environment, this form of political argument will develop new terms in which to speak about needs, welfare, jobs, the global community (themes to which I return later in this chapter). This will involve conceptual and analytic rigour to which an anodyne and sloganizing political culture is admittedly unreceptive, but it will also involve a taking of unequivocal long-term positions, based on clearly stated alternative values, such as might help to restore some life to political debate.

It is as a necessary aspect of ecological restructuring that the intervention of the State in 'the economy' might, I am arguing, win the kind of legitimacy which is already granted to government-directed environmental protection. Market relations perform a range of tasks essential in any society with a complex division of labour. We rely largely on the market to distribute income, to meet basic needs, to articulate regional and sectoral and national economies, to allocate social wealth (as 'private capital') between different branches of production. While market-like mechanisms might continue to play an important role – providing consumer choice and flexibility in the supply of commodities – in an ecologically planned economy, these central economic functions would need to be determined in directly political fashion.

Even under governments of the right, state intervention plays a part in ensuring minimum incomes and in meeting social needs which the market is ill-fitted to satisfy. I suggest below that the defence and extension of this type of redistributive and welfare provision would be part of the programme of any 'eco-social democratic' administration. Such an administration would be restraining 'market forces' by the kinds of environmental legislation mentioned above, and would also, as it took more ambitious steps, seek to regain public control over key resources (defined in ecological as well as economic terms). The eventual form of an eco-socialist economy – whose financial basis would have broken with the 'law' of value – is an important matter of debate: I draw up my own sketch later in this chapter. The point I am making here is that the idea of an *ecological* transformation of the economy can in itself play a part in renewing the legitimacy of political interventions in the market: deprivatizations of crucial industries such as energy, support for 'uneconomic' but ecologically sound agricultural reforms, and even – what now seems an unlikely project – a programme of 'eco-contraction' in some branches of industry (automobiles, defence, agro-chemicals). We should bear in mind that *capitalist* restructuring has had, and is having, violently disruptive effects on local and sectoral economies: steel, coal-mining, ship-building, merchant shipping. If the Right has been able to win political support for these in the name of a rather abstract 'realism', can an ecologically informed socialism not aspire to creating a consensus for its own very different objectives? Of course, this latter type of transformation would aim to involve workers in any plant subject to politically determined run-down in the creation of alternative forms of work and production, along the lines established in the well known Lucas and Vickers workers' plans.

What kind of public authority might press for and implement an ecological restructuring? It would have to be a 'strong State' in terms of its regulatory and financial powers, though the image of a centralized, unitary body, appropriate in the sphere of finance and macro-planning, must be complemented by an image of a multitude of local bodies at once more powerful and more accountable than what we have today. In so far as this accountable, ecologically progressive 'strong State' was clearly seen to challenge the often remote and autocratic centres of power which now determine the economic fate of entire communities, its political authority would be in principle legitimate. However, that legitimacy would depend also on its political forms, objectives and practices.

It follows that the campaigning organizations and parties that might argue for an eco-socialist transformation should at the same time be seeking to define and extend the sphere of democracy and participation generally: by arguing for electoral reform, for a clear legal definition of civil and political rights, for the whittling away of official secrecy, for open government, for the creation at every level of new forums of popular debate. On these questions, there is a body of radical tradition, not confined to the Left, which green and eco-socialist campaigns can endorse and embody.[7] Beyond this, an active green/eco-socialist movement can itself become a focus and agent of authentic political argument, a mobilization of dissenting opinion. E . P. Thompson, decrying the nullities of consensual party-political discourse, has also insisted on the potential of 'alternative culture', of 'dissent', to disrupt those nullities:

> What's generally appalling . . . is . . . the definition of what 'politics' is . . .
> For example, all political discourse must assume that we're agreed on the need for economic growth . . . But across the world people are asking questions of *why* and *where?* Do we have the right to pollute this spinning planet any more? To consume and lay waste resources needed by future generations? Might not nil growth be better, if we could divide up the product more wisely and fairly?
> . . . A body-politic without an enquiring spirit to ask *where* and *why* is like a car bumming down a motorway with an accelerator pedal but with no more steering than can just keep the car on the lane.[8]

The 'enquiring spirit' of the ecological movement can perhaps play its part in creating a new period of real political questioning, and in giving birth to a social awakening like those embodied in some other moments of our history: Chartism, the successive struggles for extension of the franchise (including its extension to women), the wide popular mobilization in support of the welfare reforms of the 1945 Labour government,[9] the vital work of popular education and consciousness-raising performed by the women's movement and the anti-nuclear movement of recent years. To the extent that it can do this – a matter dependent, not just on the quality of its ideas, but on the energy it puts into their diffusion – it can ensure that the necessary ecological reforms it will be advocating will appear, not as the impositions of bureaucracy, but as the enactments of democratic purpose.

Needs, welfare, equality

I remarked in my discussion of utopian socialism (in chapter 3) that the green movement can rightly see itself as expressing a pervasive ambivalence about 'progress', but added that the political articulation of this ambivalence was a difficult business. The question of needs – do we have 'true' and 'false' needs?; 'needs' as opposed to 'wants'?; do the artefacts of rich consumer societies represent a fulfilment, a distortion, a betrayal of human needs? – is the focus of this complex discussion,[10] which runs back into the history of socialism, as can be seen if we compare two passages from nineteenth-century writing.

The first is from Morris's *News from Nowhere*. In it, Hammond the historian is looking back on the 'last age', the age of industrial capitalism which preceded the utopia of the novel:

> In the last age men had got into a vicious circle in the matter of the production of wares. They had reached a wonderful facility of production, and in order to make the most of that facility they had created (or allowed to grow, rather) a most elaborate system of buying and selling, which has been called the World-Market . . . They created in a never-ending series sham or artificial necessaries, which became . . . of equal importance to them with the real necessaries which supported life. By all this they burdened themselves with a prodigious mass of work merely for the sake of keeping their wretched system going . . . They . . . forced themselves to stagger along under this horrible burden of unnecessary production . . .[11]

Morris's utopia depends essentially on Hammond's distinction. In the post-industrial England of *News from Nowhere*, a polar contrast in this respect with the dystopia of *Brave New World*, all 'sham' necessaries have been dispensed with. The landscape has been freed from blighting industrialism, and the burden of labour enormously lightened. And the 'real necessaries' – plus a few undeniable luxuries, of which fine claret (imported, naturally, from French vineyards) is the most striking – are now made with care and artistry.

To this may be contrasted Marx's account of the 'civilizing

influence' of capitalist industry in creating new, 'wholly social' needs:

> Capital's ceaseless striving towards the general form of wealth drives labour beyond the limits of its natural paltriness, and thus creates the material elements for the development of rich individuality . . . *Natural necessity in its direct form has disappeared*; because *a historically created need has taken the place of the natural one.*[12]

It would be easy, and in part justified, to say of this formulation that in it Marx expresses a productivist and triumphalist 'Enlightenment' attitude (is he not celebrating the 'conquest of nature'?) which has dominated much socialist theory and practice, and which we now have to transcend or anyway qualify. A green or eco-socialist politics of need will in terms of its *values* surely owe more to Morris than to this aspect of Marxism. We may conclude (as Bahro concludes about a rather similar passage from the *Communist Manifesto*) that 'we can no longer share the spirit' in which Marx was wont at times to celebrate the progressive role of capitalist industry.[13] Nonetheless, the Marxian *analysis* should detain us, at least in one crucial respect: Marx is clearly right in speaking of the *replacement* of one set of needs ('satisfiers'[14] may be a more precise term) by another.

Morris distinguishes between 'real' and 'sham' needs, between what 'supports life' and what is 'unnecessary', as if that distinction was also essentially a distinction between an earlier or original set of needs and a later 'artificial' *accretion* (and this is the root of his essentially regressive utopianism). However, much of what is quite recent in the life of a modern village in the rich countries (sewage and drinking water, electricity, means of transport) is necessary in a day-to-day sense for the village's inhabitants. It has *replaced* such earlier necessities (themselves historically developed) as the well, the dungheap, the smithy. Many of these needs/satisfiers (even in the earlier phase) admittedly went and go beyond what is needed for mere biological survival, but Morris does not and we cannot equate 'life' with survival – though whenever we say this, we should remember all those who do live within the terms of that brutal equation. It is also true that the inhabitants of today's village use or own many other commodities (private cars, foreign holidays, central heating in the loo) which it is rather easy to class as 'wants' or 'luxuries'. Nonetheless, at any moment the forms (or satisfiers) taken by quite ordinary and basic needs will be newly developed: everyday social reproduction incorporates a large quantum of historically new needs.

Thanks to the fundamental role played by the market as the distributor of 'purchasing power', which includes the power to purchase food and shelter and warmth, even those engaged in the production of quite blatantly 'artificial' needs (giant furry toys, asparagus flavoured crisps . . .) will moreover see the marketing and consumption of those 'needs' as the condition of their own more basic satisfactions.

Let us now turn from this discussion, which brief as it has been serves to emphasize the complexity of the question, to a more direct survey of the kind of politics of need which ecological argument entails.

The green movement is impelled to develop such a politics because the 'natural necessity' whose eclipse Marx vaunted is set to *re*appear as ecological scarcity, and because the 'World-Market' decried by Morris has issued in extremes of affluence and indigence.

> Ultimately human needs have to be defined as those levels of health and autonomy which are available to all people in all societies, given present and probable future levels of resources. . . . The logic of the politics of human need is irrepressibly global in scope: no group of humans can have their basic needs excluded from consideration . . . Finally, ecological considerations dictate that the need-satisfaction of future individuals . . . be taken into account in the present allocation of resources.[15]

In this historical context Jonathon Porritt is right to insist that we must make the 'unequivocal judgement' between different needs (as I would put it: he speaks of 'wants' and 'needs'; 'genuine' and 'artificial' needs);[16] for the prospect of unlimited and undifferentiated extension and proliferation of needs is

70

untenable. Moral and philosophical argument, such as he himself develops, must inform that judgment – and the green movement, in so far as it promotes such argument, should shame all those who can speak only of 'growth' within an inherited first-world structure of needs.

In the end, value judgements have to be reached and negotiated and made effective in the society as a whole, not just as individual moral choices (though they are necessary too). Greens and eco-socialists have accordingly not only to raise the question of needs in itself, as a political question, but to develop political/economic frameworks within which the transformation of needs can be advocated and made real. In this, two aspects are particularly important. We have to emphasize the contradictory nature of our present satisfactions, and the frustrations (often of non-material needs) that these entail. And we have to make the satisfaction of an agreed set of basic needs an economic priority: here, we move into the questions of welfare and equality.

I argued above (in chapter 3) that in speaking of 'particular' and 'general' interests we should not forget that 'interests' are often mutually contradictory: one and the same person or group can experience needs that conflict with each other. Let us consider at a little more length one instance that I gave, that of the different needs of users of city streets, recently discussed by Roger Higman of Friends of the Earth and SERA. Higman reports on the transformation lately taking place in some northern European towns, especially in Holland (where 'socialist cities like Delft, Groningen and Maastricht have been in the fore'), as traffic planners stopped giving unthinking priority to the needs of motorists:

> They started by linking the three aims of a better community, a safer road system and a more pleasant environment, into a concept the Dutch have called *Woonerf* – the living street.
> Non-travel uses of a street were recognised and promoted. The environment was redesigned to make it more conducive to community development. Vehicle speeds were lowered to walking speed using devices like road humps to allow children to play without fear. The pavement was abolished and people encouraged

71

to walk all over the road which was broken up with trees, flowerbeds and benches . . . Preventing through traffic and slowing down what remains helps reduce noise and pollution levels.[17]

Similar developments, increasingly common in Germany, are also in the offing in a few British cities. Here is an ideal focus for local green/socialist action (and collaboration across party lines). It also makes concrete the general question of needs, their contradictions, and the hierarchy among them. In one sense, and this is important, we see the assertion of the needs of one *group* – which incudes a disproportionate number of women, children, and older people: the 'economically inactive' – against those, previously dominant, of another (comprising a disproportionate number of men[18] and of the relatively well-off and powerful). But this is *also* an assertion of the primacy of certain commonly felt *kinds* of need (for conviviality, neighbourhood) at the expense of others (for rapid transit, 'saving of time') which are themselves widely felt: needs that may coexist within one and the same person.

Notable, too, in this example is that the obscured (perhaps only half-conscious), frustrated needs which re-emerge and claim satisfaction as rat-run becomes *Woonerf* ('living street'), are non-material needs: they cannot be manufactured, marketed, bought. They are even anti-market, anti-economic needs: we can all see the use of cars travelling quickly – a businessperson might be hurrying to a conference, a journalist to a briefing – but where is the use of kids playing ball or old people gossiping in the sun? These non-economic needs register, in the language of mainstream politics, mostly as deafening silence.[19] This silence is somewhat comically broken in Labour's 1987 manifesto; on page 14 of the 17-page document we find the heading 'Towards a Fuller Life' (which comes below 'A Better Deal for Consumers') followed by the cautious admission: 'Life is not only work', and the promise: 'Labour will make provision for the co-ordination and development of leisure amenities and the leisure and cultural industries'. Ah yes: the cultural *industries*: even apparently non-economic needs can be marketed, and can provide jobs, after all.[20]

An older and wiser socialist tradition, of which Morris is an eloquent exponent (but which includes Marx too), has always seen the assertion and cultivation of the full variety of needs (needs for interesting work, more free time, safe and attractive domestic and public space, quiet and beautiful places in town and country) as the entire point of socialist transformation. Work, in such a vision, has two aspects: it is (or can be)[21] a pleasure for the worker and a means of self-realization, and it satisfies the material needs of the society – material needs which are understood to be governed by a general agreement that a comfortable sufficiency, rather than a constant expansion, is the objective of production/consumption.

Ecological constraints, and the moral imperative of moving towards less unequal global patterns of consumption, place at the centre of any radical agenda the project of defining and making a priority of agreed basic needs in rich as in poor countries. In capitalist societies, moreover, unmet needs of a quite basic kind of course coexist with unprecedented luxury consumption.

The key questions for this project are: which kinds of production and provision constitute 'basic needs'? How (the market having conspicuously failed) is priority to be assured for them? And can a political mobilization in favour of such a project be created?

Let us begin with the last question, where, in Britain, recent and continuing argument about the NHS offers a starting point. The welfare state is a tenaciously valued inheritance of the 1945 reforms, and adequate funding of free health care is seen as a priority even among liberal and some conservative opinion.[22] Ten years of aggressively market-oriented conservatism, supported by a large part (though not a majority) of the electorate, have not finally altered this. Nurses and other health care workers taking action to defend the NHS have been supported by Vauxhall workers on Merseyside and by the trade union movement at large. The Thatcher government is provoking a response, and a challenge to its priorities. In developing this challenge, it is crucial to emphasize the essential moral and political claim: the claim that, whatever else we produce/

73

consume/need, we need this first of all (and I regret that the Green Party's reasonable concern about the particular definitions of health care embodied in the NHS have sometimes obscured this central point).[23]

There are other kinds of provision – education and social services, energy, sewage services and water supply, public transport, housing, the postal service – which meet basic social needs and in which it is still reasonable to hope that the incursion of market economics, and the whittling away of provision, can be repelled or reversed. I say 'reasonable to hope': of course there can be no guarantee of success beforehand: but if we abandon *this* ground (and it is ground where party-political divisions and ambitions should not obscure the fact that very many 'centrist' voters will join hands with the Left), if we yield *these* historic gains of social democracy to the forces and the ideology of the market, then we have absolutely no hope of making any kinds of substantial, or even insubstantial, interventions in the play of 'economic forces'.

An eco-reforming social democratic administration would not only restore lost provision. In areas where social and ecological needs mesh together (energy and transport are the most immediately important), it would intervene with new priorities and methods, aimed at a sustainable, environmentally benign meeting of needs. This must mean, not only encouraging certain technologies and kinds of service (insulation and investment in renewable energy, railway electrification and the opening of new lines), but ending or discouraging others (nuclear power, the use of private cars). Such interventions are both politically and economically more difficult than simply providing *more*. Still, they could be initiated within the 'mixed economy', with costs met by taxation (mainly of the rich) and also by transferring expenditure away from 'defence' and the nuclear industry. Fiscal measures can also begin the move towards *equality* – which is connected directly with 'basic needs': in so far as they are not provided free, then essential goods have to be paid for, and are less available to the poor. Food, in Britain, is affordable even to the least well off, but housing, an equally basic need, is certainly not. As inequalities are removed, the 'effective demand' of those who can make few demands increases: the structure of needs changes even within the framework of the market: there is less demand ('need') for Rolls Royces and yachts, more demand for reasonable housing.

Here, in the matter of equality, the difficult relation between class politics and eco-politics is most intimate and potentially fruitful, for any prioritization of agreed 'basic needs' such as a non-repressive ecological programme would involve must to some extent represent also a move away from the disparity between privileged luxury and deprivation. However, the goal of equality for all – including women (and men) involved in childcare, the old, those not working in currently profitable sectors – is not reached by the strategy of winning back for workers in successful capitalist firms that proportion of the value of their labour of which they are presently deprived. It involves an appropriation and distribution by the society as a whole of the whole social wealth produced. And while fiscal measures may initiate the process, its completion takes us beyond the market. So also does a pursuit of welfare, of basic needs, as *priorities*. For while there may be an actual or potential public agreement that the meeting of certain social needs should come *before* the proliferation of needs in general, the fiscal means by which welfare is funded, and which might suffice to begin an expansion of the sphere of welfare, actually *reverse* the terms of that public perception. Production in general, in the 'wealth-creating sector', becomes the resource base for the particular production/services which we agree that we all need. In Morris's terms, we 'stagger along' under the burden of overall capitalist production, and produce an ever-growing pile of 'sham necessaries', to raise revenue for 'real necessaries'.[24]

Let me conclude this section by offering some thoughts about the 'model' for a non-market economy prioritizing the meeting of needs.[25] There would be, first of all, and building both politically and materially on the inheritance of the welfare state, an expanded range of services and commodities to meet needs for education, health care, social services, basic infrastructural requirements (water, sewage), energy, transport, housing (where local programmes to improve the housing stock would be developed). Some at least of these services and commodities would be provided without any money transactions being involved.

This sector would enjoy the first call on social labour. Within it, norms applicable to *all* employment would be established concerning hours of work (and this would be a major determinant of total social production). These norms would involve a recognition that 'domestic labour', and especially the care of children and the elderly, the ill, disabled people, is itself a meeting of the most basic needs. Those who did such work would also be able, if they so wished, to participate in other kinds of work, with flexible 'job-sharing arrangements' facilitating this, but anyone who chose to do only 'domestic labour' would be regarded, and recompensed, as a worker.

Levels of 'pay', or social income, would also be established in this sector and would apply to all types of employment including those in the 'market-like' sector (see below). In my own view these 'rates of pay' should be based on the principle of all work being equal, with the proviso that certain heavy or tedious or especially demanding occupations might have shorter hours. This 'rate of pay' would also be made to retired people, to students, and to whoever could not find employment or was physically unfit for it – though where people with disabilities wished to work they would have a right to do so. Some proportion of this socially agreed income would also be payable in respect of children.

This planned meeting of social needs would be under direct social and political control. The 'law of value' would have no existence in it. Ecological objectives would inform every part of it (and it might, certainly in the short and medium term, include 'cleaning up' existing environmental damage). In resource-intensive areas (energy and transport especially), this ecological perspective would include a commitment to bringing UK levels of resource consumption down to levels compatible with global justice.

Beyond this, and again evolving out of what we now have, a 'market-type' sector would produce a range of commodities and services between which people would choose according to preferences. Some of these – food, clothes, furniture – themselves fall into the category of 'basic needs', but needs of a kind where choice between different kinds and proportions of consumption is valuable. ('Social income' of course includes provision to 'buy' all these basic needs as well as some 'wants'.) Other commodities and services – holiday travel, record players, drink, tobacco, books etc. – are not needs which we all share, and here the feedback of market-type mechanisms is an effective means of allocating social labour to meet demand, and of encouraging the necessary expansion and contraction of the productive and retailing enterprises concerned. This is the rationale for the pseudo-market and the use of money. The monetary form, moreover, as opposed to some utopian visions in which the citizenry simply help themselves from a cornucopian socialist abundance, implies the possibility, which in ecological terms is a necessity, of exerting collective control over levels of *overall* individual consumption. Basic needs are met, and there is then the choice between luxuries, rather than the endless proliferation of 'new needs'.

But this market would differ fundamentally from the capitalist market. The law of value would not apply as the determinant of rates of pay, which (as I have argued) would already be determined socially. Accumulation and profit would not be possible: the accruing of a money surplus in a particular sector or enterprise would be an indication that, other things being equal, it might expand, or that other similar enterprises might be set going: but this money, which might be used as an 'investment fund' (though in my view decisions to 'invest' labour and materials in a new enterprise would be best taken in directly social/political ways, often at local level), would not in any case be the property of the personnel of the enterprise. Accounts of firms in a particular town or region would be subject to supervision by civic bodies. If a lot of cash had piled up, then there could be some public festivity at which this was joyfully burned.

In the absence of profit, the rationale for private ownership would have gone, though what forms of ownership/management/ control were best in each case would vary. In strategic large-scale industries (agriculture, mass production) forms of direct social control and planning would seem appropriate, but in other cases cooperative or 'small business' set-ups might be

77

preferable. In any case, the incentive for participating in economic activity would lie in the 'altruistic' pleasure of meeting needs – and this, surely, is *already* an important motive, alongside monetary ones, not only for many workers but also for many capitalists.[26]

Where direct control by representative bodies was not established, ecological and internationalist objectives would be reflected in the legal circumscription of economic activities: the prohibition, curtailment or regulation of kinds of production collectively identified as harmful, wasteful, or damaging to the interests of poorer countries.

Above all, this pseudo-market would not be a 'wealth-creating sector', on which social needs would be fiscally 'parasitic'. On the contrary: its place in the hierarchy of social labour would be explicitly subordinate, though that part of its production (in agriculture, clothing and the like) which met basic needs, and did so in an egalitarian context, would obviously thrive.

Jobs

The preceding remarks have extensive implications for the pattern of employment in an eco-socialist society. Rather than exploring these implications further, I want to return to the present, and make some observations on the arguments and ideological/value positions which greens and eco-socialists should bring to their discussion of employment. This is particularly crucial in a context where 'jobs' risk becoming for the labour movement what profits are to the capitalist: the sufficient justification for any production whatsoever. How often does one open the paper or turn on the radio or T.V. and find some pernicious project such as Star Wars presented in terms of the 'jobs' it will provide?

Even in green and eco-socialist publications it is not unusual to read such formulations as 'caring for the Earth is the biggest job-creation scheme ever'; 'wave power . . . would lead to many new jobs in shipyards'; 'much of our waste could be successfully and profitably recycled; and, in doing so, we could create many new jobs'; or, from the white collar union TASS: 'Invest in a clean environment. Investment means jobs'.[27] Such formulations do imply a distinction between socially and environmentally useful and harmful work. But they leave intact the assumption that we suffer from a 'lack of jobs'. Here, as in the notion of 'economic growth', a one-dimensional argument has to be replaced by a more differentiated and complex approach. Otherwise, and despite attempts to specify useful rather than useless/harmful work, the pressure for 'jobs' per se remains a powerful stimulus to overall economic expansion.

A developed modern economy, with its material and technical resources and its skilled workers, can meet without difficulty the basic needs of a lifestyle unprecedented in its level of physical comfort and security. Ecological and internationalist arguments enforce the conclusion, developed at length in the preceding section, that what is now needed is a stabilization, perhaps at a more frugal but still ample level, of this material standard of living. In this framework, necessary work can be equitably shared, and social income distributed by non-market mechanisms.

This is the argument as it applies to 'demand': to the structure of social need which employment and labour satisfy. What also needs developing, in green argument, is a critique of the subjective need for work. Much work is surely not a good *in itself.* This is among the points made in a polemical article by Howard Wagstaff and Tony Emerson:

> Socialism is about production for need. We should be starting from the question, what should the economy be producing to meet people's needs? Then, what would be involved in producing it, and how can we spend as little time as possible in factories and offices, so that we can get on with the real business of living? . . . People are expected to spend 40 hours of about 48 weeks for over 40 years of their lives at the grind, as long as there's profit to be made out of it. Instead of trying to turn these values on their head, the arguments espoused by the labour leaders faithfully reproduce them.[28]

The relegation of 'jobs' to their place in the hierarchy of subjective needs, the assertion that many forms of work are unpleasurable and should be performed as quickly as possible in order to allow us more free time: this is one element in the necessary eco-socialist argument (and the only coherent response, as Gorz emphasises, to the work-eliminating potential of automation).[29]

At the same time, many in the green movement argue for the development of technologies that are 'good and satisfying to work with',[30] and generally for the promotion of kinds of work that *are* rewarding in themselves. This is very much part of Morris's vision in *News from Nowhere*, and Robin Cook cites Morris in arguing that an ecological socialism would foster 'work practices that recognise the dignity of workers and their need for self-expression at the workplace'.[31] There is evidently a contradiction between this perspective and that of 'saving time'. The contradiction is not a matter of incoherence, but of counterposing two different solutions *each* of which would have a part to play in a collectively planned ecological economy. The balance between 'saving time' (that is, reducing social labour) and working pleasurably, but longer; the kinds of production in which one or the other is the appropriate aim; how those who do intrinsically dull work might be recompensed (in terms of shorter working hours), or how everyone might be called on to do their share of such work – these would be themes of political debate in an autonomous, non-market society. They need to be canvassed as themes now, even though we cannot at present resolve them collectively.

It is also possible to argue now for the simple objective of a shorter working week. 'The social productivity of human labour is now so great that a vast reduction in working hours is already here upon us', as John Ure has observed in his criticisms of Labour's Alternative Economic Strategy:[32] and although this productivity, in the capitalist market, is by no means devoted to the meeting of basic needs, many workers are already paid far more than is necessary for the enjoyment of a comfortable material standard of living. For many people, the option of working less is already attractive and feasible even without an overall reorientation of production. An eco-reformist administration might well introduce legislation to assure employees the legal right to reduce their hours of work while retaining security of employment, and to oblige many jobs to be made available to job-sharing applicants. It is surprising that such proposals do not figure in the current Green Party manifesto (where 'job-sharing [and] more part-time arrangements' are however advocated as one advantage thought to flow from the introduction of the Basic Income Scheme).[33]

It would be better, of course, if the objective of shortening the working week were central to trade union strategy, and a real advance in this area may depend on this. The 1983 programme of die Grünen does include a commitment to a 'gradual reduction in the working week (initially to 35 hours)', but this has been an area of tension between the party and the trade unions.[34] In Britain, although a shortening of hours is sometimes an issue in disputes (it figured in the Post Office dispute in late 1987 and is a stated long-term objective of several unions, including ASTMS), it can hardly be said to be a priority. The 1987 Labour manifesto included policies on extending rights to early retirement and on protecting the rights of part-timers, but said nothing about the objective of a shorter working week. In many sectors, levels of overtime remained high throughout the recession. Gorz, assembling evidence to show that there is a widespread popular desire for a shorter working week, identifies the 'reservations, indeed hostility' which this desire often encounters in trade union circles as both mistaken and short-sighted:

> We should bear in mind that a lot of the men and women today who want to work, but not for 39 hours a week all year round for the rest of their lives, are quite simply opting for a lifestyle which is likely to be dominant in 10 years time. Should the union movement reject or condemn them in the name of an obsolete religion of work, it will only be harming itself . . .
>
> By refusing to organise or give a voice to those who want more time for themselves right now, unions are only cutting themselves off from part of their own base, and strengthening the employers' power at their own expense.[35]

Internationalism and autarky: a note

The Labour Party's 1987 general election manifesto (*Britain Will Win*) devoted a bare three paragraphs, at the very end, to 'the horrors of famine and poverty in many countries'.[36] It is almost twenty years now since Julius Nyerere addressed his *Appeal to the Socialists of Europe*, in which he insisted that the benefits from unequal global exchange accrued to

> the national economies of the rich nations – which include the working class of those nations. And the disagreements about division of the spoils, which used to exist between members of the capitalist class in the nineteenth century, are now represented by disagreement about division of the spoils between workers and capitalists in rich countries.[37]

If they are to vindicate their emancipatory and egalitarian claims, socialist and social democratic parties in first-world countries have to develop economic strategies which explicitly and as a priority confront the issue of global inequality and how to redress it. The green movement may not have fully developed such strategies, but green argument has been willing to accept the challenge of Nyerere's *Appeal*, and to recognise what development economists such as Gunnar Myrdal have long been saying: that 'without very radical changes in the rich countries' patterns of consumption, all talk of a New International Economic Order will remain pure bluff'.[38]

Let us be clear about what this implies. It does not mean that we are in a 'zero-sum game' in which any and every type of first-world consumption is at the expense of poorer countries. It does, however, rule out, in the name of international solidarity, first-world 'economic growth' as usually conceived, which envisages an expanded consumption, in rich countries, of raw materials and energy that are in finite supply and of which per capita consumption in the developed industrial societies is already very much in excess of that in the Third World. And it entails the recognition that present forms of global interdependence, derived from the colonial past, are forms of structural inequality rooted in violence. Few individuals – very few in the present generation – may feel that they have been directly involved in creating this 'world market', but all of us in Western Europe are its beneficiaries, in an economic and ecological relation which surely involves a moral responsibility. And here, as in the sphere of environment and resources, we find ourselves enjoined to replace the notion of 'growth' and to argue, in already-rich societies, for forms of economic development which envisage *lower* levels of material consumption in many respects.

This is the underlying orientation of an eco-socialist internationalism, and is now leading to the formulation of specific development policies. I do not intend to offer, here, what could in any case only be a cursory discussion of these policies, but rather to say a little about the political/ideological terms in which this new internationalism is presented in relation to existing transnational institutions and to inherited, British, ideas of nationality. In particular, it is worth looking critically at the notion of *self-reliance* or *autarky*.

There are some strong arguments for greater self-reliance. Poor countries evidently need to develop domestic processing and manufacturing industry (rather than exporting raw materials and cash crops for processing elsewhere). There is often a clear, if unmet, need to increase production of food for home consumption. This involves relations of power and property within as well as between nations, and of course a nominally 'domestic' processing industry which is actually owned by a Western transnational corporation may do little enough to develop a Third World national economy. Nonetheless, there is a clear international dimension. It is their indebtedness which so often constrains even progressive Third World governments to maintain export levels well above what they would ideally choose. A principled first-world strategy for writing off that indebtedness must then lead, at least temporarily, to a reduction in trade, and thus to a more autarkic or self-reliant mode for first-world countries too, since these would no longer be importing raw materials and cash crops, and exporting arms and other manufactures, in the former quantities.

A strategy of 'delinking' also has attractions for first-world countries attempting to set out on an 'alternative development' path of their own. The search for competitiveness on the world market strongly determines the direction of economic and technological change, and supplies a ready ideological armoury for use against the proponents of ecological, low-growth strategies, as Wolfgang Sachs notes:

> When every other argument fails, the stick of declining inter-national competitiveness is used to silence the protagonists of fundamental change. Recent debates in Germany provide us with telling examples: even the government recognised that the fast-breeder reactor promised to be an economic disaster, but it nevertheless decided to complete construction so as not to 'fall behind' in technical know-how; a moratorium on genetic research because of uncontrollable consequences, as requested by the Greens, was dismissed with laughter, since Germany could not afford to 'drop out' of the international biotechnology race . . .
>
> The protagonists of high tech have a vocabulary much like the boulevard press reporting from the Olympic Games: 'Germany (or France or Italy) is falling behind, we are overtaken by foreigners, let's hurry to join the race, to catch up and take the lead!'[39]

And of course this kind of economic nationalism (not exactly unknown in the British Labour movement) is plainly irrational once we recall that exactly the same kinds of rhetoric are being heard all over 'Europe open for business'. Rather than enter a race in which there can apparently be only one winner, it appears reasonable to 'drop out' after all.

Autarkic strategies can be defended, finally, at the most general level, by arguing that there are two broad conceptions of how we might move towards an internationalist eco-development. Either one thinks in terms of a 'semi-autarky', at least, in which particular nations exercise political sovereignty in the transfor-mation of their own economic life; or else one thinks in terms of the collective development of new international structures (the kind of 'socialist world market' envisaged, for instance, by the *New Left Review* editors in their dialogue with Bahro[40]). But this second development, apart from the pertinent question of whether we can truly imagine a transnational initiative of the kind which would be needed to bring it about, may not be desirable in itself. This is the argument of Boris Frankel, in an interesting exchange with Alec Nove: 'global material production and interdependence', argues Frankel, must, however it is organized, 'provide the basis for a nightmare'. In this argument, the very volume of world trade, the specialized orientation of local economies within it, and the impossibility of exercising local democratic supervision of its operation, are held to outweigh whatever notional benefits might come from a socialist 'world central plan, or a world of soviets, or a world of market socialist nations still competing with one another'.[41]

These, then, are arguments for an autarkic, self-reliant image of eco-development. In my own view, reduced volumes of clearly redundant trade (apples, butter, television sets, cars all traded between countries that produce their own supplies of these commodities) would make ecological sense, as would objectives of greater self-sufficiency in energy, staple foods, and raw materials (where re-use and recycling have a large role to play).

However, the invocation of national self-reliance is a matter for caution, both ideologically and in terms of practical realism. Ideologically, it must be recognized that any such invocation, in Britian, will have, as part of its sub-text, an appeal to British nationalism. The image of 'Britain standing alone' can be summoned in support of radical causes (rejection of cruise missiles, withdrawal from NATO or the EEC), but it draws in its wake a history and a still enduring assumption of imperial and racial privilege. Reverberations from this inheritance easily interfere with an overt message of egalitarian internationalism. A more autarkic ecological-economic policy – or rather, a policy of what Frankel calls 'semi-autarky': greater self-reliance where this is appropriate, mutually beneficial trade where it is not – should properly be presented, not as a unilateral option, but as a possible objective of altered relations *between* nations (both Third World and developed industrial nations).

Practically, we know that we have to reckon, not with a series of discrete national economies, but with a world market and a world financial system, in which Britain, like most of its EEC partners, is deeply involved both as a trading nation (with 22 per

85

cent of GNP currently exported[42]) and as a financial centre. Opinions vary as to how effectively any single country could act to retrieve a measure of financial and industrial autonomy.[43] Socialists and eco-socialists will urge that the uncertainty of success cannot forever inhibit us from striking out, alone if need be, on a new path – and they might add that a country such as Britain has a far more highly developed industrial and technical base than did Russia in 1917 from which 'eco-socialism in one country' could be constructed. However, an ecological-egalitarian restructuring of world trade – which must imply controls on transnational corporations and financial institutions, and envisage eventually replacing them as managers and agents of the world market – is certainly a project that stretches, and exceeds, the political grasp of single nations. If we believe, as I do, that 'semi-autarkic' goals themselves, if they are to benefit poorer countries, must be accompanied by that kind of active international restructuring, then we must think in terms of parallel and reciprocal moves by many nations. We should perhaps envisage the same kinds of process as might bring about nuclear disarmament: a combination of unilateral and multilateral measures, with green movements and green-inclined governments supporting one another across frontiers.

There is a further practical objection to the autarkic perspective, analogous to that which I raised as part of my critique of the green emphasis on 'the local economy'.[44] Even within the relatively homogeneous economic space of capitalist Europe, we find wide divergences in population density, land-use, scale and type of industrial development. Some of these divergences are due primarily to historical development, but they also reflect differences in soil fertility, availability of local raw materials, and so on. It is one thing to object to the particular kinds of interdependence which the market has created between these specialised regional and national economies, but it is another to suggest that some degree of interdependence will not and should not persist – between, say, agricultural exporters such as Denmark or the Irish Republic (with respective population densities of 117 and 44 people per square kilometre) on the one hand, and more crowded industrial and manufacturing countries such as the UK (244 per square km.) or the Federal Republic of

Germany (248 per square km.) on the other – even if the present set of market relations were replaced by a conscious strategy of greater self-reliance. Again, the notion of 'autarky' seems neither feasible, at least in the medium term, nor necessarily appropriate.

It is worth observing, finally, that the EEC, while its fundamentally capitalist orientation is not in doubt (and is quite evident, currently, in the preparations made for the single market of 1992), cannot be regarded as an entirely reactionary entity by libertarians and environmentalists in Britian. A number of judgements, for instance on corporal punishment in schools, have shown that 'European' opinion is often more enlightened than British on matters of individual rights. Environmentalists often quote EEC directives and recommendations, for instance on bathing beach pollution or levels of nitrate in groundwater, to highlight the relative backwardness of British legislation. British recalcitrance over acid rain is another, blatant item of evidence.

This does not make the EEC and the European Parliament bastions of libertarian and ecological enlightenment, but it does mean that Greens in this country should be wary of seeing their national political space as an especially favourable ground for eco-politics. As we saw in chapter 1, and as will be further illustrated in the next (and last) chapter, green politics is in some respects a Western European movement. Other EEC countries, since most of them have some form of proportional representation, have Green MPs and Euro-MPs where Britain has none: indeed Paul Staes, the Belgian Green MEP, has often raised in the European Parliament matters of concern about which British greens have asked him to speak. Any greening of British political culture is likely to take place as part of a wider change, involving other EEC countries, and aiming, not simply to create a more decentralised and regionally/locally autonomous Western Europe, but also to bring into being new relationships between the national entities, and between them, jointly and separately, and the nations of Eastern Europe, the Third World, and elsewhere.

5

Red and Green:
A New Radical Politics?

An effective eco-socialist movement must ultimately involve trades unionists and workers, but it cannot be expected to arise (as some would still see a revolutionary Marxist politics arising) from the pursuit of workplace- and wages-based interests. Like the anti-nuclear movement, the ecology movement has developed political arguments, single-issue campaigns, and educational work, with the aim of canvassing support from the society at large. Again as with the anti-nuclear movement, there has probably been an expectation that the most sympathetic audience will be on the Left: but as political ecology has defined itself as green politics, this has entailed a difficult and in part conflictual relation with established Left groupings. We have seen that the green movement, while it may share with socialism an (implicit or explicit) anti-capitalism, hardly envisages traditional mainstream socialist objectives in the sphere of production and consumption, and these differences of aim, along with important cultural and sociological differences, have led to the formation of Green parties distinct from, and in electoral opposition to, the parties of socialism. Meanwhile many of these latter parties (and certainly the British Labour Party) are ideologically and electorally in retreat, and the socialist aspect of their politics is ever more effectively concealed within a social democratic ideology and programme.

It is in the interplay between these formations – established social democratic parties and small but often dynamic Green parties – that the intellectual dialectic of red and green finds its clearest organized expression. In Britain, there have recently been signs (the May 1988 Green and Socialist Conference in London, the substantial green input to the Chesterfield Socialist Conference process) of a broader and more amicable dialogue.[1] If this is to lead, as it is to be hoped that it will, to the creation of a specifically eco-socialist political presence, the process is likely to involve ruptures as well as new alliances.

In my own opinion, developed in this chapter, we need to keep a double aim in view: the creation of a political force which integrates ecological limits and priorities in a truly socialist programme can only come about as part of a broader realignment, entailing the break-up of the Labourist coalition, but this will have disastrous electoral results unless we can successfully campaign for a long overdue reform of Britain's unrepresentative first-past-the-post electoral system.[2] We need electoral reform to ensure that a broadly progressive social democratic coalition, committed to the welfare state and to some measure of redistributive taxation, can regain a parliamentary majority; for the Labour Party, which itself once *was* that coalition, cannot confidently expect to reclaim the necessary votes from the centre parties. But we also need electoral reform so that a distinctively socialist party, which in the 1990s must surely be an *eco*-socialist party, can emerge from within the Labourist coalition.

It is against that strategic background that I now turn to make some party political observations about the Greens and the Labour Party.

The Greens and the Left

In Britain, the Green Party (and its precursor, the Ecology Party) has held a 'neither left nor right' position. The electoral rivalry between the Greens and all the other parties has been paralleled and vindicated by an ideological/theoretical distinction between 'the politics of ecology' and the 'politics of industrialism', with the latter thought to embrace both capitalist and socialist societies. The distinction is developed in *Seeing Green* by Jonathon Porritt, the best-known and most effective exponent of green ideas in Britain in the early 1980s.[3] In 1984, in a debate which raised important general issues, Jonathon Porritt defended the majority decision of the European Green Parties, at their first joint congress (Liège, 1984), that – despite the urging of die Grünen – they would not give their support to the Dutch 'Green Progressive Accord', an *ad hoc* alliance set up for the forthcoming Euro-elections between the Communist Party, the Radical Party and the Pacifist Socialist Party. The Green Parties, he argued, should insist on what was specific to their own political vision, and should avoid getting drawn into a broader coalition:

> To . . . work to establish minimum green criteria is not divisive: it is an essential part of our responsibility. To take to our bosom all those who've learned to manipulate people at the level of 'shallow ecology' would mean the comprehensive failure of what greens throughout Europe are trying to achieve . . .
> We [in the Ecology Party] have thought through our role within a growing green movement, and we intend to stick to it: consistently and often without the reassurance of tangible, easily quantifiable success, to take the fullness of green politics to all and sundry.[4]

Here is an assertion both of the ideological independence of green politics (the reference to 'shallow ecology' implicitly invokes the 'new paradigm' of 'deep ecology'[5]), and of the unique educational responsibilities of the Green parties.

The claims made for the novelty and self-sufficiency of 'ecology' as political discourse have undoubtedly been too large: there has been a disturbingly unhistorical aspect to what David Pepper calls the 'rejection of the "old politics" by greens', with its 'elevation of the idea of "newness" to an almost sacred principle.'[6] Porritt is however right, in my view, to suggest that a distinct political identity has been crucial to the educational and cultural impact of the Green parties: had those parties allowed themselves to be drawn into a subordinate and marginal relation to 'actually existing electoral socialism', they would have found great difficulty in articulating clearly their basic message about ecological limits.

Beyond that basic message, the Greens have also contributed to a general reorientation of critical and utopian thinking. A green 'politics of consumption' or lifestyle politics is developing, which calls on us to accept that 'the consumer' (each one of us) is something more than a passive victim of the capitalist expansion of needs; and this points towards a non-electoral politics of change, working at the level of personal responsibility rather than of structure and system. Saral Sarkar, an Indian journalist who worked for a time in the office of the Köln Greens, has written interestingly on this:

> Demands must be made not principally on the state (though these must be made too) but mainly on ourselves . . . That way we should have to start here and now, in our everyday lives – and it is something millions of people, the masses, *can* do.
> . . . If for example we want to get out of the motor car society (something the greens want, according to their manifesto) then all we need to do is get out and walk. . . .[7]

Argument of this kind, which parallels the feminist insistence on the interweaving of 'personal' and 'political' dimensions of life, challenges socialist conceptions which regard changes in production and in relations of power as the sole nexus of political-historical struggle.

Yet in the end the Greens, too, are wanting change of a structural kind: the rationale for the existence of political parties lies in the belief that *collective* action is necessary, and that beyond whatever changes individuals can and should make in their particular lives, there needs to be a restructuring of social and economic relations. Here, I have argued throughout this essay, the ecological critique comes up against many of the forces and structures which socialists have contested, and here accordingly the future development of eco-politics is likely to involve an acceptance of what was denied at Liège in 1984: that elements of the Left are the natural allies of the Greens.

Indeed it can even be argued that some small progressive parties, in particular the Dutch PSP (Pacifist Socialist Party), have anticipated the greens' concerns with such themes as non-violence, the environment and the development of socially useful production.[8] This was the line taken by die Grünen in the Liège debate: the new Dutch Green party, de Groenen, could

91

not claim a monopoly of green/ecological argument (the Germans argued), and it was wiser to see the development of green politics as involving *both* the promotion of new Green parties *and* the seeking of broader alliances between greens and other progressives. Of course, debate about relations between political ecology and socialism has been lively within die Grünen, as too has debate on the quesiton of relations between the party and the west German SPD. From the beginning, die Grünen, as too has debate on the question of relations between dimension of their political foundation ('Our policy is . . . guided by four basic principles: it is ecological, social, grassroots-democratic and nonviolent'[9]). However, it is one thing to accept that ecological policies have to be set in a broader framework, and another to agree on what that framework should be: notoriously, die Grünen have been prey to complex internal divisions over economic and social policy and over the question of whether they should promote, or 'tolerate', or refuse coalition or co-operation with the SPD.[10] It is worth observing that despite these divisions, they have continued to receive the support of electors, increasing their share of the popular vote by some 2.5% between the Bundestag elections of 1983 and 1987.[11]

Following the disagreements at Liège, die Grünen chose to remain outside the European Green confederation, though they continued to cooperate informally in joint projects with the other parties. In 1987, they successfully applied to join the coordination, though still regarding its exclusive nature with suspicion: one reason they gave for wishing to work within the common structure was their desire to 'contribute to a better collaboration between different Green, alternative and radical parties'.[12]

The delegation from die Grünen which came to Britain in May 1987 was evidently committed to this tactical and political line, for its members visited, not only the UK Green Party conference at Newcastle, but also several figures and organis-ations of the British Left (SERA, the NUM, the Socialist Society and others). German Euro-MP Jakob von Uexküll suggested to the Greens at Newcastle that, having now established a clear political identity, they need no longer feel the old defensiveness about seeking dialogue with other progressive groups:

> What Die Grünen are saying to you, from their own experience, is that you are now strong enough – you should be self-confident enough – to go out and be more open to cooperating with other people. You should be less afraid of being tainted or categorised than you were a few years ago . . . Your independent position, standing beyond the left–right spectrum, which you felt was so important, was indeed important; but now it's time to move beyond that position, towards some of those people who are ready to come a step towards you.[13]

This is very much my own view. As it has evolved from its primarily environmental focus, the green argument has been concerning itself with many questions (the Cold War and the blocs, the limits of GNP as a measure of real social wealth, the impact of feminism on productivist notions of 'the economy') which also engage the attention of a growing number of socialists. Green positions have often been closer to the ideals of the Left than those put forward by the Labour Party front bench: compare, for instance, the arguments on nuclear weapons, dealignment, and foreign policy in the 1987 election manifestoes of the Labour and Green parties. It follows that green activists, far from being defensive, can claim to have been part of a movement that has taken the initiative in some important areas, and has much to offer to any wider coalition of radical groups.

The Labour Party: 'new realism' and the marginalization of the Left

In Britain, an engagement with socialism, in the electoral and party-political sphere, means an engagement with the Labour Party. Given the British electoral system, socialists have as a rule accepted the necessity of forming part of Labour's broad coalition, which includes social democrats as well as many of the various strands and factions of the socialist and Marxist Left.

Attempts at setting up electorally independent radical alternatives – the ILP, the Communist Party, and more recently the Green Party – encounter the undeniable fact that they tend to split the progressive vote, and the corresponding reluctance of many progressive voters to support them: such attempts in the past have proved short-lived. Whether this pattern will continue is an open question, but for the present, Left elements in and around the Labour Party (those who are either members or critical but nonetheless electorally faithful supporters) provide, along with the Green Party and the broader green movement, the most important constituency in which eco-socialist ideas can be further developed and campaigned for. I am not suggesting that only socialists or the Labour Left are interested in or receptive to general information and argument on environmental and ecological themes: on the contrary – such argument and information is reaching a wide audience, beginning to influence policy and programmes across the mainstream political spectrum,[14] and, by encouraging people of diverse backgrounds and preconceptions to look critically at contemporary economic rationality, is potentially a significant radicalizing force. But it is to a closer alliance of red and green movements, emerging from the Left and the Greens, that we must look for the development of the arguments, fusing social and ecological critiques of capitalism, which will best be able to mobilize this potential radicalization.

The Greens, I have just been arguing, are perhaps ready to move beyond an earlier neither-left-nor-right stance, and to open a dialogue with the Left. The founding, in January 1988, of the Association of Socialist Greens, some of whose activists took part in the subsequent Green and Socialist Conference and in the second Chesterfield Socialist Conference, indicated that some Green Party members at least were ready to respond to Jakob von Uexküll's call to 'be more open to cooperating with other people'.[15] In the dialogue now beginning, two areas of difficulty are apparent. The first is, so to speak, intrinsic to the very project of red-green co-operation: differences of opinion, of political culture and outlook, of social class and education, which clearly exist between greens and Labour Party socialists, make dialogue tense and agreement uncertain. However, it is of course the intention of dialogue to explore such differences, and in my own judgement they need not prevent the formulation, over the next few years, of an eco-socialist 'minimum programme'. A difficulty much harder to surmount lies in the subordinate position which that part of the Left now engaged in dialogue with the greens occupies inside the Labour Party coalition.

This subordination of the socialist Left to the social democratic Labour leadership, and the recurrent tension to which it has given rise, has recently been charted by Hilary Wainwright in *Labour: A Tale of Two Parties*. One of its consequences, particularly relevant when we are considering the role of political parties and movements in the development and communication of radical, new or unfamiliar arguments, has been a 'crisis of political representation' which the Left, within Labour's coalition, has suffered 'because its ideas . . . have no direct platform':

> The left in the party sees its arguments refracted and diverted as if through a prism, by internal party conflicts. The refracted view is then enlarged by the more powerful prisms of the media, so that the original ideas survive only in a sub-culture of left newspapers, public meetings of the converted and the occasional late-night programme on Channel 4.[16]

Even when they have been able to win conference support for radical policies, and have been overwhelmingly supported by constituency activists, the Left cannot ensure that they are argued for effectively. The fortunes of the non-nuclear defence policy have illustrated this. Potentially, this policy might have been made the focus of a much wider campaign, with connections made with the civil nuclear industry (which, in 1987, Labour was also – nominally – opposed to); with the environmental and human costs of nuclear testing world-wide;[17] with the nature of the Cold War, the prospects that this will begin to thaw, and the part which a non-nuclear government in Britain might play in building a new detente. Instead, the policy was inserted, incoherently, into an unchanged framework of rhetoric and assumptions about the immutability of the bloc system and of the Soviet threat, the unshakeable loyalty of Britain to NATO, the self-evident desirability of 'strong defence'. Now, in 1988, it appears probable that the front bench would like to ditch the anti-nuclear commitment altogether, and is deterred from doing so only by anxiety about getting the party conference to swallow what would, after all, be an entirely undemocratic decision.

What underlies the reluctance of senior Labour politicians to campaign for the more radical policies which Labour activists, particularly on the Left, would often like to see foregrounded by the Party? There are no doubt genuine differences of political opinion, on defence as on other issues. There is, especially in economic policy, the wish to balance the interests of different trade unions – not an unreasonable wish, but one which has prevented a clear taking of positions on, for instance, nuclear power, and which is also questionable, as I argued earlier, because of the one-dimensional definition of 'interests' which trade union politics sometimes embodies.[18] There is also an element of electoral calculation: the Labour front bench seems sometimes to be listening with one ear to Party members and Party policies, and with the other to the opinion-poll mediated buzz of 'public opinion', as if it were equally answerable to each constituency. This last element has become more explicit of late, with Labour's policy review conducted in a spirit which has at times seemed not unfairly epitomised in Bryan Gould's dictum: 'Market research will tell us what people want and then our job is to show that we are the party that can provide it.'[19]

The notion that politics is about 'giving people what they want' is not self-evidently absurd or incompatible with democratic socialism. But Gould's formula obviates two aspects or functions of political organization which greens and socialists will regard as crucial: the function of stating and defending positions of principle (such as a refusal of nuclear weapons or of support for apartheid) which cannot depend on calculations about popular support; and the function of attempting, through argument and through the provision of information and evidence, to *alter* people's views about what they want. The latter aspect is especially important when 'what people want' is contradictory:

an ensemble of needs and desires that may conflict with one another, with the needs of other people, or with ecological constraints. This complex reality cannot be represented in the one-dimensional language of market research, and no political fix can satisfy all these wants. Labour's 'new realism', well-grounded as it may be in electoral arithmetic, is objectionable not only because it silences radical and socialist ideas, but because it lacks complexity and honesty, acceding to and reinforcing a trivialisation and evacuation of political language.

And yet: the electoral arithmetic remains. And the British electoral system gives it particular constraining power. With PR, a drop of ten per cent in a party's share of the vote translates into a 10 per cent drop in seats. But in our first-past-the-post system, a drop from 35 per cent (about Labour's current level of support) to 25 per cent might entail a massive loss of representation,[20] from which it could prove difficult or impossible to recover. The conscious advocacy of what are known to be minority positions, in the belief that they can, in time and after serious campaigning, attract substantial support, is precisely what is thus pre-empted by the electoral calculus. Hence what Richard Kuper calls 'the fudge that characterises Labour politics, a fudge that is almost built into the electoral system at present.'[21] The appeal to the middle ground, presented (with some immediate justification) as electorally indispensable, constrains the Left to silence at election times (moments of most sustained public political debate); strengthens the Right in every disagreement; and has helped to render socialist ideas more and more marginal to mainstream politics over the last four decades.

Realignment?

There are two obvious strategies for the Left, in this situation. One is to persist in the struggle, difficult though it is, for control of the 'commanding heights' of Labour politics, or at any rate to continue to mount campaigns which, if they fall short of success (as Tony Benn's 1988 leadership challenge obviously will), nonetheless maintain a socialist pressure from below, give rank-and-file socialists in the party something to identify with, and maybe keep alive some kind of public language of socialism – though this, as Hilary Wainwright notes, will indeed be 'refracted and diverted . . . by internal party conflict' and by the media presentation of it.[22]

The other strategy, which is not necessarily incompatible (at least in the short term) with the first, is to search for a broader realignment, drawing together socialists inside and outside the Labour Party, reaching out to 'new social movements', and so establishing a new socialist presence both allied to and independent of Labour. This is what Wainwright envisages when she writes of a 'process of refounding the left', in which 'the left would be part of two coalitions: the coalition of Labour and the coalition of radical socialism which reaches beyond Labour'.[23] And this, clearly, has been the political strategy behind the Chesterfield conferences, in whose organisation both Hilary Wainwright and Tony Benn have been involved.

It is within this broader process that dialogue is now beginning between red and green. I would like to conclude with some remarks on the scope and nature of the realignment that we might, and should, be seeking.

First of all, we must address as wide a constituency of politically engaged people as possible: and it should be borne in mind that the collapse of the Alliance and the founding of the SLD will have left some radical Liberals wondering where their future lies. Members of the Green Party have been engaged in discussion with some disaffected Liberals, and Brig Oubridge, a former Green Party co-chair, has argued that the Alliance (and its successors), like Labour, has been a coalition of radical and conservative elements, and that

> the problem which faces the radical elements in both the Labour and Liberal parties is that they are in the wrong coalitions. The contradictions between the radical and conservative factions in both the Labour Party and the Alliance are too deep to be resolved or papered over, and in their present forms neither can present a coherent radical alternative to Thatcherism.
>
> That radical alternative does exist, however, and its direction is undoubtedly green.[23]

It is admittedly open to question whether current members of the Liberal Party would form part of an explicitly eco-socialist movement of the kind that I believe we need (though the first principle held in common by Greens and radical Liberals is, they state, 'a desire for a classless society').[24] What is certain is that there are people here who should be involved in dialogue, and for whom the themes of social justice and ecological sustainability are politically important.

Secondly, any Left grouping founded as a challenge to Labour's drift towards the centre must be prepared, practically as well as psychologically, to cut the electoral tie with Labour. This will not inevitably be necessary: it is not inconceivable that the Labour Party itself might (perhaps if they lose a third, or fourth, election under 'realist' leadership?) move decisively to the Left, under pressure from a new radical coalition and from its own constituency workers. But it is equally possible – if the Left finds itself decisively outvoted at successive conferences (on the strength of the trade union block vote), and/or if Neil Kinnock succeeds in winning an election – that Labour will stay firmly on the centre-right. In that eventuality, a credible socialist grouping must be prepared to establish a new electoral organization.

But, thirdly, in readiness for that contingency – and also for the alternative possibility that, having won control of the Labour Party, the left would then see massive defections (including defections of sitting MPs) and a permanent split in the old Labour coalition – a 'refounded Left' must be arguing and campaigning for PR, and specifically for a form of PR (like the German system) which allows proper representation to minority parties. PR is obviously attractive to the Greens, and also to socialists who see it as affording opportunity for the establishment of a fully committed socialist presence which 'could begin to transform political life in Britain':[25] it must, I am suggesting, be on the agenda of all those who are seeking a realignment on the Left. But it also has important attractions for liberals and democrats generally, both because of its intrinsically more representative nature, and because (thanks to this) it can ensure the re-establishment of a centrist politics committed to some measure of support for the Welfare State and some measure of redistributive taxation. These modest goals are not what socialists and eco-socialists aspire to. But they are better than Thatcherite conservatism, and they are also closer to the wishes of most people in Britain. And electoral reform, it must surely be agreed, is an essential element in the programme of any campaigning group concerned with democratic rights and liberties generally.

Fourthly, and finally, a 'refounded' socialism must, as it has hitherto been too slow to do, take up the challenge of ecology and of the Green Parties and green movements. Both the negative, constraining limits of ecological responsibility and the positive, utopian critical thinking which that responsibility provokes are essential aspects of any serious political reawakening: as I have argued all through this book. And, as I have also argued, it is within the terms of socialism, critically re-examined but still adhering to many of its founding principles – need before profit, equality, social/political control over economic life – that the ecological challenge can best be understood and met. Raymond Williams[26] recognized the difficulty of working towards a socialism refounded in ecological terms, but he also insisted on its potential strength:

> There are already kinds of thinking which can become the elements of an ecologically conscious socialism. We can begin to think of a new kind of social analysis in which ecology and economics will become, as they always should be, a single science . . .
>
> The case for this new kind of enlightened, materially-conscious, international socialism is potentially very strong, and I think we are now in the beginning – the difficult negotiating beginning – of constructing from it a new kind of politics.

Notes

1: Ecology Crisis and Green Politics

1. See World Commission on Environment and Development (chaired by Gro Harlem Brundtland), *Our Common Future* (Oxford 1987), pp. 228–9. Earlier summaries, discussions and reports include: Harold J. Bartlett and Chandler Morse, *Scarcity and Growth* (Baltimore 1963); Donella H. Meadows and others, *The Limits to Growth* (the 'Club of Rome Report') (London 1972); and – especially recommended – William Ophuls, *Ecology and the Politics of Scarcity* (San Francisco 1977). See also the bibliographies in these works.

2. *The Limits to Growth* (1983 paperback ed.), p. 23.

3. Rudolf Bahro, *From Red to Green* (London 1984), p. 179.

4. *Our Common Future*, pp. 1–2.

5. See the works referred to in footnote 1 above and cited in their bibliographies. Ophuls' book is particularly valuable because alongside much empirical/statistical material, it introduces methodological and analytic questions (such as those involved in understanding the dynamics of exponential growth) fundamental to long-term economic tendencies.

6. Dennis Clark Pirages, in Pirages (ed.), *The Sustainable Society* (New York 1977), p. 3, citing work by Frederick Dewhurst.

7. *Our Common Future*, p. 174.

8. *Ibid.*

9. *Ibid.*, p. 195. 'Renewable' energy is distinct from nuclear energy because the latter depends on finite reserves of uranium: even the use of fast-breeder reactors cannot indefinitely overcome this constraint (quite apart from safety objections).

10. *Ibid.*, p. 170.

11. *Ibid.*, pp. 189–92.

12. See the discussion in chapter 4 below.

13. *Our Common Future*, p. 14.

14. *Ibid.*, p. 9.

15. *Ibid.*, p. 3.

16. *Ibid.*, p. 2. See also Steve Elsworth, *Acid Rain* (London 1984).

17. *Green Line*, 58, p. 7, 'Prague's Silent Spring', citing articles in *The Guardian*, *New Society* and *East European Reporter*. The article refers to the ecological initiatives taken by Charter 77 and SZPOK in the wider context of the Gorbachev reforms: for some further discussion of this, see the section on 'Actually Existing Socialism' in chapter 3 below. *Green Line* is a non-party green movement magazine produced in Oxford (34 Cowley Road, Oxford OX4 1HZ).

18. *Our Common Future*, p. 178.

19. *Ibid.*, pp. 2–3.

20. F. Capra and C. Spretnak, *Green Politics* (London 1984), p. 223.

21. This point is developed below, especially in chapter 2 (with particular reference to the British Labour Party).

22. *Our Common Future*, p. 2.

23. William Ophuls makes clear, schematically but persuasively, the fact that we face a range of 'ecological' options, not only in his book (cited above) but in his contribution to the collection, *cit.*, edited by Pirages. There are important divergences between the ecological projections found in the various works cited in note 25 below. To take a particular point, the writings of Alvin Toffler are cited approvingly by both André Gorz (in *Paths to Paradise*, London 1985) and by Capra and Spretnak (*ibid.*, p. 194), whereas Murray Bookchin (*The Ecology of Freedom*, Palo Alto 1982, p. 333n.) treats him with considerable scepticism.

    The general point that I am making in this part of my argument – that ecology on its own does not define a politics – has of course been made elsewhere, for instance in André Gorz's *Ecology as Politics*, Boston 1980 and by Hans-Magnus Enzensberger in 'A Critique of Political Ecology', *New Left Review*, 84.

24. See Raymond Williams, 'Socialism and Ecology' (pamphlet), Socialist Environment and Resources Association (London n.d.).

25. 'Deep ecology' is the title of two books. One is by Bill Devall and George Sessions (Utah, 1984); the other is edited by Michael Tobias (San Diego, 1984). The quotation from Brian Tokar is in his *The Green Alternative*

(San Pedro, Ca., 1987), p. 27: see my brief review of the book in *END Journal*, 31. The final phrase is from Capra and Spretnak, *ibid.*, p. xix. Further, and in my view equally untenable, use of the term 'paradigm' is made in the essay by Dennis Clark Pirages in Pirages (ed.), *cit*. An English essay in ecological philosophy is James Lovelock, *Gaia* (Oxford 1979).

26. On these characteristics of the Green Parties, see below.

27. Porritt, *Seeing Green* (Oxford 1984), pp. 216–17.

28. Bookchin, *ibid.*, p. 315. I must make it clear that my discussion engages only with certain aspects of Bookchin's work, and makes no pretence to criticise it as a whole.

29. *Ibid.*, p. 216.

30. *Ibid.*, p. 342.

31. *Ibid.*

32. *The Winter's Tale*, Act IV, sc. iv. 'Mend', in the penultimate line of the passage quoted, has the sense of 'improve upon'.

33. *Romeo and Juliet*, Act II, sc. iii.

34. Bookchin, *ibid.*, p. 28.

35. *Ibid.*, p. 24.

36. Porritt, *ibid.*, p. 3.

37. For an account of this, see Capra and Spretnak, *ibid.*, pp. 16 ff.

38. The first slogan is that of the French Greens; the second is from the *Programme of the German Green Party* (London 1983), p. 6; the final phrase is from Jonathon Porritt, *Seeing Green*, pp 216–17.

39. In his Preface to the German Greens' Programme (in English translation), *ibid.*, p. 4.

40. Accounts of the Green movement and Green Party have focused on West Germany. They include the study, *ibid.*, by Capra and Spretnak, which emphasises the aspects to which I refer here. A more sociological account is in E. Papadakis, *The Green Movement in West Germany* (London 1984). Recently published, and offering a fully documented 'inside view', is Werner Hülsberg, *The German Greens – A Social and Political Profile* (London 1988).

41. It was in the summer of 1985 that the present author completed a study of 'Green Politics and Socialism in Britain', commissioned by the UN University (unpublished, available from the author). Information in the present chapter whose source is not otherwise indicated is based on that paper.

42. Chiefly the UK Green Party newsletter *Eco-News* and the Oxford-based monthly *Green Line*: see notes below for detailed references.

43. For a round-up of UK Green Party results in both local and general elections of 1987, see *Eco-News*, 35, p. 9.

44. For an account of the French situation at the March 1986 elections, see *Green Line*, 41, p. 17; on Spain, see *Eco-News*, 35, p. 9; on the Netherlands, see Green Line, 44, pp. 4–5, and also the discussion in chapter 5 below.

45. See *Eco-News*, 34, p. 5, report by Sara Parkin (International Liaison officer of the UK Greens).

46. *Eco-News*, 35, p. 3 (Austria) and p. 2 (Switzerland).

47. See *Green Line*, 58, p. 7 and *Eco-News*, 35, p. 3.

48. *Green Line*, 41, p. 16 and 47, p. 4; *Eco-News*, 35, p. 9.

49. Hülsberg's comments are in his article in *New Left Review*, 162, p. 97. For electoral details, see *Green Line*, 47, p. 3 and 44, p. 4, and *Eco-News*, 35, p. 2.

50. See the 1987 election manifesto of the UK Green Party, pp. 24–26.

51. Pamphlet available from the UK Green Party.

52. For Japan, Australia and New Zealand, see the notes in *Eco-News*, 34, p. 3. For the US situation, see Capra and Spretnak, *ibid.*, pp. 193 ff., and Brian Tokar, *ibid.* On Eastern Europe, see below, chapter 2.

2: Socialism in an Ecological Perspective

1. See especially the closing section of Raymond Williams *Towards 2000*, (London 1983); and also Williams' pamphlet for SERA, 'Socialism and Ecology' (London, n.d.). Boris Frankel's *The Post-Industrial Utopians* (Oxford 1987) includes valuably detailed critiques of Gorz and Bahro as well as more general discussion of several issues relevant to any eco-socialist programme: I draw on it below, especially in chapter 4. *Red and Green*, ed. Joe Weston (London 1986), is a Left critique of the Green movement which is marred, in my view, by simplification and neglect of major questions, and by a failure to respond to or even cite the programmatic and ideological writings of the Green Parties. Other socialists who have written on green politics include Peter Tatchell and Jeremy Seabrook; F. E. Trainer (see his *Abandon Affluence*, London 1986) and Robin Cook, whose two articles in the SERA magazine *New Ground* are cited later in the present chapter.

   The continental thinkers whom I refer to have published the following books and essays (apart from those by Gorz and Bahro already cited): Lucio Magri and Luciana Castellina contributed essays respectively to *Exterminism and Cold War*, E. P. Thompson and others (London 1982), and a collection published by Verso, *Socialism on the Eve of the Year 2000*; Erik Damman's *Revolution in the Affluent Society* (London 1984) combines a grasp of socialist/Marxist economic argument with a commitment to personal moral responsibility.

Among recent British symposia and essays on the future of socialism which virtually or completely ignore all the questions posed by the ecology crisis and the green movement are the following: Ben Pimlott, ed., *Fabian Essays in Socialist Thought* (London 1984); Gavin Kitching, *Rethinking Socialism* (London 1983); James Curran, ed., *The Future of the Left* (Oxford 1984); Martin Jacques and Francis Mulhern, eds., *The Forward March of Labour Halted?* (London 1981) (in the latter volume, however, there is a fine essay by Raymond Williams, to which I return below).

2. Geoff Hodgson, *Labour at the Crossroads* (Oxford 1981), p. 215. This conception of an unproblematic alliance between labourism and 'other movements' is of course widely held: see for instance Tony Benn in the volume ed. Jacques and Mulhern, cited in the previous note, p. 89: 'The Labour Party must align itself with the women's movement, the black movement, the environmental movement, the peace movement . . .'.

3. A recent analysis of the tensions between socialism and social democracy in the Labour Party is Hilary Wainwright, *Labour: A Tale of Two Parties* (London 1987).

4. David Selbourne, *Against Socialist Illusion* (London 1985), p. 14. He quotes successively from G. D. H. Cole (summing up what he takes to be Keir Hardie's view), F. Hayek, Neil Kinnock and Tariq Ali.

5. R. Bahro, *From Red to Green* (London 1984), p. 235.

6. *Ibid.*, pp. 235–6.

7. J. Porritt, *Seeing Green* (Oxford 1984), p. 226.

8. A not unjustifiable response in itself: see my further comments in the section on Class, below.

9. In Karl Marx, *Revolutions of 1848*, ed. D. Fernbach (London 1973), p. 95.

10. See my article in *New Socialist*, 44, pp. 36 ff.

11. B. Taylor, *Eve and the New Jerusalem* (London 1984), 'Introduction'.

12. See Porritt, *Seeing Green*, p. 225; Bahro, *From Red to Green*, p. 235; Robin Cook, 'Towards a Socialist Ecology', *New Ground*, 14, p. 31.

13. E. M. Wood, *The Retreat from Class* (London 1986), p. 17 (not that I agree with all Wood's criticisms of Gorz, let alone with the general argument of her book: see the section on Class, below, for some further comments).

14. *News from Nowhere*, Lawrence and Wishart ed., (London 1968), p. 295.

15. Kate Soper, 'Rethinking Ourselves', in *Prospectus for a Habitable Planet*, ed. Dan Smith and E. P. Thompson (Harmondsworth 1987); see pp. 202–3.

16. Boris Frankel has some apt criticisms of Bahro's utopianism: see Frankel, *ibid.*, e.g. pp. 56–7, and elsewhere. For my comments on Green economic theory and 'the local economy', see chapter 3 below. Other dimensions of the present argument about 'regression', 'progress' and utopia are taken up in my discussion below of needs and of work (in chapter 4).

17. The very fact that they have constituted themselves as electoral parties underlines the acceptance, by the Green Parties, of the liberal-democratic tradition, even if both the UK and the West German greens stress the limitations of that tradition and the need for a more participatory, community-based political life. In the wider green movement, there is an anarchist/decentralist/libertarian tradition which is more sceptical about electoral politics: most issues of *Green Line* illustrate this, and see several of the essays in N. Albery and M. Kinzley, eds., *How to Save the World* (Wellingborough 1984).

18. See Scilla McLean, ed., *How Nuclear Weapons Decisions are Made* (London 1986), esp. pp. 222 ff., outlining the role both of the Nuclear Planning Group and of the 'High Level Group'.

19. See, for instance, the *New Ground*/GLC supplement in *New Ground*, 6. See also Brighton Council's environmental charter of 1988.

20. The Green Party of the UK produced a critique of the major parties' policies shortly before the 1987 election (*Green Politics: Fact and Fiction*, London n.d.). Written by Paul Ekins (though not published under his name), this makes some of the points developed here, but is in my own view a rather superficial critique. On Labour and the economy, see p. 11.

21. See the 'quote' beneath the picture of Neil Kinnock on the back cover of the 'Charter' (*Labour's Charter for the Environment*, London, n.d.).

22. *New Ground* 14, p. 22. See also Victor Anderson and Jeff Cooper, 'Good Intentions', *New Ground*, 8, p. 16.

23. Nuclear power is passed over in silence (!) in the *Charter for the Environment*: there is a brief section on 'toxic and nuclear waste' (p. 21) which never says where radioactive waste comes from. The 1987 Manifesto does contain a vague commitment to 'gradually reducing Britain's dependence on nuclear energy' (p. 7), however.

24. *Seeing Green, ibid.*, p. 120: Porritt goes on to outline this more complex position: 'in the developed world, there will be limited growth in certain sectors of the economy, even though the overall base will no longer be expanding; in the Third World, there will have to be substantial economic

growth for some time, though with much greater discrimination as regards the nature and quality of that growth . . . '.

25. On GNP and 'alternative economic indicators', see chapter 4, below, where I mention the work of TOES in developing such 'indicators'.

26. See the Labour ·Coordinating Committee's pamphlet 'There is an Alternative' (London n.d.); and A. Glyn and J. Harrison, *The British Economic Disaster* (London 1980).

27. Tony Benn interviewed by Eric Hobsbawm, in *The Forward March of Labour Halted?*, p. 91, 95. Cf. the comments of Victor Anderson and Jeff Cooper in *New Ground*, 6, p. 16: 'The issue now has become: what form should rebuilding the economy take? Which sectors should get the money made available for new investment? Keynesian generalisations about expanding the economy completely fail to answer these questions.'

28. Labour's 1987 manifesto, p. 1, p. 3.

29. As can be determined, for instance, from figures in Glyn and Harrison, *ibid.*, p. 5.

30. See chapter 1, above, for references to the Brundtland report; and A. Gorz, *Paths to Paradise* (London 1985), pp. 92 ff.

31. Lucio Magri, 'The Peace Movement and Europe', in New Left Review/E. P. Thompson and others, *Exterminism and Cold War* (London 1982). See p. 132. Thompson's endorsement of Magri's perspective (he quotes, to be precise, a slightly later passage from the same paragraph as I cite, beginning with the fourth sentence printed in my text) is on p. 347 of the same volume. Magri writes as a socialist who sees the new movements, including ecologists, active in the peace and anti-missile campaign as beginning to grasp, in a 'genuinely utopian' if still 'confused' manner, the full dimensions of a peaceful order: see p. 133.

32. See especially chapter 3 below.

33. *New Ground* (Spring 1984) p. 12. Cf. Jonathon Porritt's comments on p. 12 of *Seeing Green* (Oxford 1984) – but Porritt does not explicitly draw the inference, namely that Labour can only adopt ecological economic policies if it frees itself from dependence on capitalism.

34. See the discussion of employment, welfare and internationalism in chapter 5.

35. Among relevant texts, from a variety of perspectives, are: André Gorz, *Farewell to the Working Class* (London 1982); Ellen Meiksins Wood, *The Retreat from Class* (London 1986); Ernesto Laclau and Chantal Mouffe, *Hegemony and Socialist Strategy* (London 1985); and some of the essays (especially the title essay, by Eric Hobsbawm) in *The Forward March of Labour Halted?* (London 1981), ed. Martin Jacques and Francis Mulhern.

36. Jonathon Porritt, preface to *Programme of the German Green Party* (London 1983), p. 4.

37. See the 'minimum green position' on 'Economics' in *Green Politics, Fact and Fiction* (London, n.d., publ. Green Party), p. 21; and for a full discussion of the 'local economic regeneration' strategy of the greens, see the relevant section of chapter 3, below.

38. I quote from an article I wrote for *New Socialist*, 44: see p. 38.

39. Raymond Williams in *The Forward March of Labour Halted?*, ibid., pp. 148–9, italics in original.

40. *Ibid.*, p. 145.

41. *Ibid.*, p. 146. A similar point was made in an interview which Peter Tatchell gave to Jean Lambert of the (then) Ecology Party in *Green Line*: '. . . essentially free collective bargaining is about the market forces, the marketplace . . .': *Green Line*, 23, p. 14, and see my further reference to this article below.

42. Barry Maycock, in *Green Line*, 59, p. 8.

43. *Guardian*, 18 February 1988, p. 23.

44. *New Ground*, 8, p. 16. For a trade unionist's point of view, see the article by Kim Howells in Joe Weston, ed., *Red and Green* (London 1986).

45. In *The Forward March of Labour Halted?*, ibid., p. 152. See also Williams' SERA pamphlet, *Socialism and Ecology* (London n.d.), pp. 13–14.

46. *Green Line*, 23, p. 13.

47. *Ibid.*, pp. 13–14.

48. *Eco-News*, 37, p. 9.

49. I use this conventional term ('Eastern Europe') as a form of political shorthand: geographically, much of the area designated would be better termed 'central Europe', and writers such as Milan Kundera have insisted that this is also the appropriate designation in respect of cultural history.

50. F. Capra and C. Spretnak (*ibid.*, p. 73) give an account of the Berlin Alexanderplatz demonstration in which a number of Bundestag deputies of die Grünen showed their solidarity with the GDR 'Swords into Ploughshares' group. For an interesting account of the response to Chernobyl in the GDR, see Mark Thompson, 'Lines of Latitude', in L. Mackay and M. Thompson, eds., *Something in the Wind: Politics after Chernobyl* (London 1988): see pp. 106–7, 114.

51. My discussion from this point to the end of the chapter draws on two essays I have written jointly with Kate Soper. The first is to be published (under the provisional title of 'Ecology and the New Detente') in R. Falk,

G. Holden and M. Kaldor, eds., *A New Detente for Europe* (forthcoming). The second is in *Something in the Wind, cit.*, under the title 'Alternative Detente'.

On environmental concern and activity in Eastern Europe, see especially Mark Thompson's essay, *cit.* in the previous note, and see also the END briefing sheet on 'Ecology in Eastern Europe', and Michael Waller's paper on 'Autonomous Movements for Peace and the Ecology in Eastern Europe' (delivered to the National Association for Soviet and Eastern European Studies, March 1987): both these last two are available from END, 11 Goodwin St., London N4.

52. For an Eastern European 'reform perspective' favourable to the Gorbachev initiatives, see the essay by Andras Koves *A New Detente for Europe*. One western socialist who has welcomed *perestroika* in terms of its market orientation is Alec Nove, who did so in a broadcast discussion (Radio 4, *World Tonight*, 3 November 1987) of Gorbachev's speech marking the 70th anniversary of the Bolshevik revolution.

53. Thompson, *cit.*, pp. 111, 112.

54. See *ibid.*, pp. 109–10.

55. Kate Soper and Martin Ryle, in *op. cit.*, pp. 204–5.

56. On the Nagymaros dam, see Thompson, in *ibid.*, p. 110; and see also the very interesting essay by Istvan Rev (an active campaigner against the project) in *A New Detente for Europe*. His contribution (entitled 'The Anti-Ecological Nature of Centralization') discusses several of the more general themes canvassed in my remarks here.

57. See Havel's remarks in *END Journal*, Spring 1987, p. 14, where he explicitly welcomes the 'proclaimed non-ideological stance' of the green movement. See also his earlier essay (written in 1978) 'The Power of the Powerless', which anticipates many themes that have since come to the fore in green politics: the essay is reprinted in Jan Vladislav, ed., *Vaclav Havel: Living in Truth* (London 1987).

Konrad does not refer directly to the green movement in his *Anti-Politics* (London 1984), but there is some congruence between his perspective and that of Havel. It is noteworthy that Petra Kelly has recently cited Konrad in support of her own sense of what the Greens stand for: see 'Doing the Impossible', *Eco-News* 37, p. 12.

58. Personal communication from Polish participants in the January, 1988 conference preparatory to publication of the *New Detente* volume, (held at the Trans-National Institute, Amsterdam).

59. See Istvan Rev's essay cited in note 56, above.

60. R. Bahro, *From Red to Green* (London 1984), pp. 101–2.

61. G. Konrad, *Anti-Politics*, *cit.*, pp. 143–4.

62. Daniel Cohn-Bendit, author in 1968 of *Obsolete Communism: the Left-Wing Alternative*, is nowadays active in the West German Green movement.

3: Green Economics: Some Eco-Socialist Observations

1. *The Living Economy*, ed. Paul Ekins (London 1986). This was a source for economic thinking in the 1987 Green Party manifesto, which I helped to prepare. Paul Ekins was for many years a leading member of the Ecology Party/Green Party (he resigned in 1987 following an argument with his local party over tactical voting: he had shortly before this been one of a group of Green Party members who tried to establish an organisation called Maingreen, to counter what Ekins and others saw as the indiscipline and unfortunate 'image' of the Greens. (See *Green Line*, June 1986, pp. 17–19, for an account of this episode). Among Green Party members acknowledged in the Preface to *The Living Economy* are David Kemball-Cook, Sally Willington and David Chapman, Convenor of the Party's economic policy working group.

   Let me make it clear that while most of my comments on *The Living Economy* are critical, I regard both the book and the work of TOES generally as valuable political interventions in an economic 'debate' which the mainstream Left has allowed to sink into sterility.

2. For instance, in the Introduction to *The Living Economy* and in the introductory remarks of the UK Green Party's economic policy section in the 1987 manifesto.

3. *New Left Review*, 152, p. 7.

4. That many greens see themselves as anti-capitalist was the conclusion I drew from interviews I conducted for my research paper (unpublished, 1985) for the UN University on 'Green Politics and Socialism in Britain'. One of those whom I interviewed, Steve Rooney, has played a leading role in the setting-up of the Association of Socialist Greens, discussed in chapter 5.

5. *The Living Economy*, pp. 1–3.

6. A point made in the review of *The Living Economy* in *New Ground*, 13, p. 16. Penny Newsome has made some extended criticisms of the book, from a socialist perspective, in *Green Line*: see numbers 51, 53 and 57.

7. See pp. 128–166.

8. Green Party Manifesto, p. 3 (my italics).

9. Hazel Henderson, in *The Living Economy*, p. 35.

10. David Cadman, 'Money as if People Mattered', in *The Living Economy*, pp. 204–5.

11. See the discussion of Welfare in chapter 4.

12. *The Living Economy*, p. 8 (my italics).

13. A. Nove, *The Economics of Feasible Socialism*, (London 1983). Boris Frankel has some useful discussion of Nove in his *The Post-Industrial Utopians* (Oxford 1987); and see also *Radical Philosophy* 39 and 41. The uses of markets within a socialist economy (or a social-democratic economic strategy) are discussed in Gavin Kitching, *Rethinking Socialism* (London 1983) and in Roy Hattersley, *Choose Freedom* (London 1987).

14. As well as my remarks on actually existing socialism in chapter 2, see the discussion of the State in chapter 4.

15. For a discussion of how capital itself is using computerized information as the basis for planning, and of how devices such as franchising and sub-contracting are replacing former models of capitalist economic control, see Robin Murray, 'Ownership, Control and the Market', *New Left Review* 164, especially pp. 88–90.

16. Boris Frankel (*The Post-Industrial Utopians*, p. 52) advocates 'the development of a centrally, but democratically planned economy (which also includes a market-based sector)': his book has some pertinent criticisms of the failure of many eco-utopians, especially Bahro, to consider the questions of the market, planning and control of the economy (see especially pp. 45–55).

17. W. Ophuls, *Ecology and the Politics of Scarcity* (San Francisco 1977), in particular pp. 167–183.

18. *Ibid.*, p. 168.

19. *Ibid.*, pp. 168–9.

20. *Ibid.*, pp. 169–70.

21. *Ibid.*, p. 171.

22. *Ibid.*, p. 170.

23. *Ibid.*, p. 171. In his 'Bibliographic Note' to the discussion (see pp. 181–3), Ophuls cites a number of recent studies, mostly by US authors, that arrive at conclusions similar to his own.

24. *Programme of the German Green Party* (London and Connecticut, 1983), p. 6. At the time of republication in 1985, the section on 'Currency, Taxation and Finance' was 'still being revised' (p. 14), which makes it difficult to assess the extent to which the market economy still underlay the thinking of die Grünen.

ECOLOGY AND SOCIALISM

New Ground 6 contains a brief review by Victor Anderson of the 1984 die Grünen policy document 'Sinnvoll arbeiten – solidarisch leben' ('Purpose in work – Solidarity in life'): although this is said to be available in English, I have not been able to see it. Anderson states that it is 'straightforwardly anti-capitalist' and 'contains no trace of Keynesian thinking'.

25. Green Party Manifesto, 1987, p. 2.

26. Green Party Manifesto, 1987, pp. 4–8.

27. It is true that recycling and repair can themselves provide alternative employment, and are in fact more labour-intensive than manufacture: see *The Living Economy*, pp. 258–9. However, the production of more durable goods would prolong, not just the overall life of commodities, but the period during which they would run without needing repair.

28. K. Boulding, 'The Economics of the Coming Spaceship Earth', in Glen A. Love and Rhoda M. Love, eds., *Ecological Crisis: Readings for Survival* (New York, 1970); see p. 314.

29. For further discussion of a non-market economy in the present work, see chapter 4.

30. See my comments on Utopian socialism and green utopianism in chapter 2.

31. The first phrase is from the 1987 Green Party manifesto, p. 8; the second is from R. Bahro, *From Red to Green*, *cit.*, p. 179.

32. *Programme of the German Green Party*, *cit.*, p. 11.

33. *The Living Economy*, p. 266.

34. 'Ford UK supplies diesel engines to Ford Europe, and imports petrol engines from Valencia. The Fiesta assembled at Dagenham used transmissions from Bordeaux, roadwheels from Genk, body panels from Spain, and suspension components from West Germany': Robin Murray, 'Ownership, Control and the Market', *New Left Review* 164, p. 91.

35. Dauncey, in *The Living Economy*, pp. 269–70. See also Murray, *art. cit.*

36. *Eco-News*, 37, p. 2.

37. Murray, *art. cit.*, 104–5. For a fuller account of the GLC experience, see H. Wainwright and M. McIntosh, eds., *A Taste of Power* (London 1987).

38. See *The Living Economy*, pp. 226–7 and references; and references in A. Gorz, *Paths to Paradise* (London 1985), p. 117, n. 7. These give the wider background. The Green Party manifesto phrase is on p. 5. For die Grünen, see F. Capra and C. Spretnak, *Green Politics*, p. 101, quoting from the Greens' economic programme, and see their discussion there

112

and on p. 97. See also Bahro's draft for the Sindelfingen conference, in *Building the Green Movement* (London 1986), p. 38, with its (vague) commitments to 'decent minimum levels for wages' and 'unemployment benefit'.

39. *The Living Economy*, pp. 224–32, and Green Party 1987 manifesto, pp. 5–6.

40. Green Party manifesto, p. 6.

41. *The Living Economy*, p. 228.

42. The manifesto phrase is on p. 5. Greens who have expressed support for egalitarian redistribution of wealth include Jonathon Porritt (see *Seeing Green*, London 1984, p. 133), and there is a general tone of egalitarianism about the Green manifesto ('even in the richest countries poor and homeless people sleep on the pavement alongside computer and video shops': p. 2), but specific commitments and measures are lacking.

43. Green Party manifesto, p. 4. Exactly the same contradiction appears in he TOES article: see *The Living Economy*, p. 227.

44. Green Party manifesto, p. 3.

45. See Ward Morehouse, 'Universalising capital ownership', in *The Living Economy*, *cit.*, pp. 232–9. This was one of the points on which Penny Newsome focused in her critique of *The Living Economy* (see note 6 above).

46. Green Party 1987 manifesto, p. 3.

47. See, for instance, Jonathon Porritt, *Seeing Green*, pp. 131 ff; Green Party 1987 manifesto, p. 3; *The Living Economy*, p. 34. It would be more precise to say that the term 'formal economy' refers, usually, to the 'money economy', to all those exchange-based activities aggregated into GNP. However, the use of this generalizing term allows, encourages, and is perhaps even (in the case of some authors) intended to allow, a blurring of the question whether the distinctively capitalist, market features of the economy, or rather its monetarization in general, are under criticism.

48. A transfer of tax towards these resource-consumption areas is, as noted above, proposed in the UK Greens' economic programme.

49. See the discussion of welfare, below. Jonathon Porritt is alert to the dangers of this type of 'dual economy': see *Seeing Green*, pp. 131–3.

50. A Gorz, *Paths to Paradise*, p. 43.

51. *Ibid.*, p. 42.

52. *Ibid.*, p. 44.

53. See B. Frankel, *The Post-Industrial Utopians* (London 1987), pp. 65–86 on

welfare and social income in general, and pp. 83–86 on Gorz. C. Castoriadis, *Crossroads in the Labyrinth* (Brighton 1984), has a lengthy and philosophically taut discussion of the questions of needs, value and distributive justice as they are posed in Aristotle and in Marx's *Critique of the Gotha Programme*: this seemingly abstract discussion focuses the question we are concerned with here: what does it mean to *go beyond* the law of value (which, Castoriadis insists, is itself no 'law' but the institutionalization of certain ideas/relations)? See pp. 260 ff, 'Value, Equality, Justice, Politics: from Marx to Aristotle and from Aristotle to ourselves'.

54. See Howard Wagstaff and Tony Emerson, 'Wanted – A Real Strategy for Jobs', *New Ground*, 3.

4: Eco-Socialism

1. They are all mentioned either in the Green Party of the UK's 1987 Manifesto or in the document on which that is based, the continuously updated policy statement *Manifesto for a Sustainable Society*.

2. See the literature on acid rain produced by Friends of the Earth.

3. The 1987 UK Green Party manifesto recognises the problem in its energy policy, which includes a commitment to 'take measures to alleviate fuel poverty'. On the interplay of ecological and social objectives here, see A. Porter, M. Spence and R. Thompson, *The Energy Fix* (London 1986).

4. *The Independent*, 25 May 1988.

5. William Ophuls, 'The Politics of the Sustainable Society', in Dennis Clark Pirages, ed., *The Sustainable Society: Implications for Limited Growth* (New York 1977), pp. 166–8.

6. Rudolf Bahro, *Socialism and Survival* (London 1982), p. 17.

7. As I write, the *New Statesman* is enlisting a broad range of liberal and progressive opinion behind the idea of a 'charter' of rights and liberties. The UK Green Party has a strongly civil-libertarian commitment, reflected in its 1987 manifesto, which calls among other things for the enactment of a Bill of Rights which 'should at least cover the rights and freedoms enshrined in the European Declaration [on Human Rights], and would incorporate the NCCL's Charter for Civil Liberties': see p. 13, and pp. 13–16 generally.

8. E. P. Thompson, *The Heavy Dancers* (London 1985), pp. 2–4, and (for the entire article, originally a Channel 4 broadcast) pp. 1–11.

9. A mobilization recalled by Thompson in *Writing by Candlelight* (London 1980), p. 82: 'Those discussions were authentic and deeply significant . . .

in wall newspapers, in bivvies around our tanks, in supply depots, the argument was going on . . . [The soldiers] debated the principles out of which the National Health Service came . . . in the direct terms of their own civilian experience.'

10. My main points of reference in what follows are: Kate Soper, *On Human Needs* (Brighton 1981), and the passages from Marx which she cites; Jeremy Seabrook, 'Needs and Commodities', in Paul Ekins, ed., *The Living Economy*, (London 1986); Manfred Max-Neef, 'Human-Scale Economics: the Challenges Ahead', in *ibid.*; Len Doyal and Ian Gough, 'Human Need and Strategies for Social Change', in *ibid.*; Jonathon Porritt, *Seeing Green* (Oxford 1984), especially pp. 196–8; William Morris, *News from Nowhere*, Lawrence and Wishart edition (London 1973).

11. *News from Nowhere*, p. 276.

12. Marx, *Grundrisse* (Harmondsworth 1973), p. 325 (my italics), cited and discussed in Soper, *op. cit.*, pp. 111 f. See also other passages cited by her from Marx, and her discussion, especially pp. 94 f. Her argument makes clear the complex and multivalent purport of Marx's philosophical interrogation of the idea of 'need', and the closing pages of her book anticipate much of the discussion now arising in and around the green movement.

13. See Bahro, *Socialism and Survival*, p. 125.

14. 'Satisfiers': the particular historical form in which a given, trans-historic need is met. See *The Living Economy*, *cit.*, pp. 49–50. Manfred Max-Neef, p. 49, argues (the passage is italicized in the original) that 'fundmental human needs are the same in all cultures . . . What changes . . . is the form or the means by which these needs are met.' 'In every system', he continues, 'they are satisfied, or not, through the generation, or non generation, of different types of satisfiers' (*ibid.*). The problem in this admittedly useful conceptual distinction is that the felt need, the subjective want, may be for the particular 'satisfier' (for instance, for a spacious house rather than a cramped cottage) rather than being experienced simply as the 'need for shelter'. As Marx wrote (I do not have the passage to hand), hunger is hunger, but the hunger that satisfies itself with knife and fork and cooked food is *different* from the hunger of the prehistoric hunter gnawing raw meat.

15. Doyal and Gough, *art. cit.* (in note 10 above), p. 78.

16. Porritt, *op. cit.* (in note 10 above), p. 197, and for his argument in general see pp. 196–8.

17. Roger Higman, 'Reclaim the Street', *New Ground* 15, p. 3.

18. See Kristine Beuret, 'Transport: Mainly for Men', *New Ground* 12, p. 3.

19. See Soper, p. 216: 'though it is true that only a society that consciously plans to meet (i.e., decide upon/determine) its needs has entered into a political engagement with the question of needs, it is also true that a society which leaves the "planning" of its needs to the dictate of economic forces "beyond its control" is in its particular way engaged in a politics of the suppression of the politics of need . . .'; and see also pp. 217–18. See also Seabrook, *art. cit.* (note 12 above), on 'the manufacture of new forms of poverty and felt insufficiency' (p. 60), though I should say that I question the rather undialectical approach of his argument ('Money and human need belong to different realms of experience'? – p. 59).

20. *Britain Will Win* (Labour's 1987 manifesto), p. 14. I am being polemical and therefore 'unfair': much that precedes this paragraph does of course deal with 'non-economic needs'. Still, the phrase 'Life is not only work' is symptomatic, and absurd. On the matter of 'providing jobs', see below – Jobs.

21. 'Or can be': because a society might decide that certain forms of intrinsically boring 'labour-saving' work, of a mechanised/automated kind, were desirable because of the saving in social labour they represented.

22. As I write (March 1988), two successive Commons Select Committees, both with Tory majorities, have called for increased NHS spending.

23. I am thinking of the discussion of the welfare state in the Green Party brochure *Green Politics: Fact and Fiction* (London n.d.). The Greens' 1987 manifesto (see p. 10) combines suggestions for a health care system more directed towards preventative medicine with an unequivocal commitment to 'a Health Service . . . equally available to everyone and free at the time of use', but has no detailed discussion of its funding.

24. See the passage from *News from Nowhere* quoted above. Similar points about the need to free 'welfare provision' from the present relation of dependence/subordination to the market overall are made by David Blunkett and Geoff Green, of Sheffield City Council, in their pamphlet *Building from the Bottom*, published by the Fabian Society (London 1983). See also Raymond Williams, *Socialism and Ecology*, published by SERA (London n.d.), pp. 15–16.

25. My sketch here can be compared with that in André Gorz, *Paths to Paradise* (London 1985) for the theoretical basis and in his 'utopia' in *Farewell to the Working Class* (London 1982) (see note 13 to chapter 3, above). It will be seen that while I follow Gorz in distinguishing between a sphere of production for agreed basic needs and a sphere devoted to 'wants' (my term, not his), my model is different in several important respects.

26. See Paul Ekins, ed., *The Living Economy* (London 1986), for two contributions by capitalist entrepreneurs/managers concerned with non-economic business objectives: Michael Phillips, 'What small business experience teaches about economic theory' (pp. 272 ff) and Willis Harman, 'The Role of the Corporation' (pp. 344 ff). The fact that the second of these seems to me misconceived does not alter the truth that profit need not be the sole, or even the main, subjective motivation of those who manage capitalist companies.

27. See respectively Green Party (UK) manifesto, 1987, p. 4 (and a similar claim was made in the only Green Party TV broadcast of that campaign); Dave Elliott, 'Energy – SERA Triumph: what next?', *New Ground* 12, p. 11; *Labour's Charter for the Environment* published by the Labour Party, (London n.d.), p. 21; and *ibid.*, p. 4.

28. Howard Wagstaff and Tony Emerson, 'Wanted – A Real Strategy for Jobs', *New Ground* 3, p. 15.

29. A. Gorz, *Paths to paradise* (London 1985), *passim*.

30. UK Green Party 1987 manifesto, p. 4.

31. Robin Cook, 'Towards a Socialist Ecology', *New Ground* 14, p. 31. Gorz, in *Paths to Paradise* and especially in his utopian sketch in *Farewell to the Working Class*, identifies tedious, 'heteronomous' labour with the sphere of basic need, and assumes also that 'autonomous', creative work produces non-basic wants. I do not think the two distinctions (basic need/want, heteronomy/autonomy) coincide in any such harmonious manner. It is hardly possible to produce 'autonomously' such luxury goods as video recorders, or cars: and some basic needs (home-grown food; care of children and the unwell) might surely be met in a more 'autonomous' fashion in an ecological society.

32. John Ure, 'Whatever Happened to Alternative Economic Strategies', *Interlink*, 2, p. 18.

33. UK Green Party manifesto, 1987, p. 3. For some specific suggestions (only some of which correspond to my own notions) see Wagstaff and Emerson, *art. cit.* (note 28 above).

34. *Programme of the German Green Party*, London 1983, p. 12. The German Metalworkers' Union waged a long struggle for a shorter working week, of course; but there has since been disagreement within *die Grünen* and between them and some unions concerning the question of whether shorter hours should also mean lower wages. See F. Capra and C. Spretnak, *Green Politics* (London 1984), p. 23 and p. 90.

35. Gorz, *Paths to Paradise*, p. 107, p. 110; and see pp. 101–110 *passim*. The article from which this section of the book is taken was first published in the journal of the *Confédération Française des Travailleurs*.

36. Labour Party manifesto, p. 16. Policies of the UK Green Party will be found on pp. 24–6 of their 1987 manifesto.

37. Quoted in Erik Damman, *Revolution in the Affluent Society* (London 1984), p. 28.

38. Quoted in *ibid.*, p. 28.

39. Wolfgang Sachs, 'Delinking from the World Market', in Ekins, ed., *The Living Economy*: see pp. 335 f., 334. For a discussion of the advantages of a relatively more self-determined trading strategy for poorer countries, see, in the same volume, Frances Stewart and Ejaz Ghani, 'Alternative Trading Strategies' (pp. 323 ff.).

40. See Bahro, *From Red to Green* (London 1984), pp. 179–80.

41. See *Radical Philosophy*, 39, p. 33, and see also Alec Nove's contribution in the same issue. Frankel develops the same theme in his *The Post-Industrial Utopians* (London 1987), esp. pp. 134–5.

42. Sachs, *art. cit.*, p. 336 (1981 figure: comparative figures for France, Italy and West Germany are 15, 26 and 22 per cent respectively.)

43. For a recent assessment, see David Gordon, 'The Global Economy: New Edifice or Crumbling Foundations?', *New Left Review* 168. On trade and the transnational corporations, attempts to control the activities of the latter (such as the 'Vredeling directive'), and the coordinated response of the multinationals themselves, see the brief but informative discussion in *The Living Economy*, pp. 339–44, as well as the articles cited in note 39 above.

44. See chapter 3 above.

5: Red and Green: A New Radical Politics?

1. Sponsors of the Green and Socialist Conference included Tony Benn and Peter Tatchell from the Labour Party and Jean Lambert and Brig Oubridge from the Green Party. The eco-socialist submission to Sheffield, co-ordinated by Andy Porter of SERA, was prepared by a group (including the present author) similarly drawn from both Green and Labour Parties.

2. I do not wish to enter into a technical discussion of the type of PR system that should be advocated: but clearly a German-style AMS (alternative member system, with one vote for the constituency MP and one for a 'list' from which the eventual proportions of the legislative body are proportionally 'topped up') is preferable to STV (single transferable vote) systems which tend to favour the centre and marginalize minority parties,

though less so than the first-past-the-post system. For a socialist case for PR, see R. Kuper, 'Two Cheers for PR', *Interlink* 2, p. 2.

3. Porritt played a major role in writing the Ecology Party's 1984 manifesto, *Politics for Life*. On 'industrialism' versus 'ecology', see his *Seeing Green*, (Oxford 1984), p. 216.

4. See *Green Line*, June 1984, p. 15; and see also, in the previous issue, the account by Roland Clarke, to which Porritt's article is a reply. A fuller account of this debate can be found in the research paper (1985, available from the author) which I wrote for the UN University.

5. See notes 23, 25 and 27 to chapter 1 for the background to the phrases 'deep ecology' and 'new paradigm'.

6. See Joe Weston, ed., *Red and Green* (London 1986), p. 116.

7. Saral Sarkar, 'How? How? How?', *Green Line*, October 1985. On 'system/ structure' as against personal responsibility, see also the letter from Steve Dawe of the Association of Kent Green Parties in *New Ground*, 15, pp. 7–8.

8. See Roland Clarke's report of the Liège meeting in *Green Line*, May 1984.

9. *Programme of the German Green Party*, (London and Connecticut, 1983, 1985), p. 7.

10. The account given in F. Capra and C. Spretnak, *Green Politics, cit.*, is valuable but marked by a persistent anti-Left bias. It can now be supplemented by Werner Hülsberg, *The German Greens – A Social and Political Profile* (London 1988). See also Hülsberg's articles in *New Left Review*, nos. 152 and 162.

11. See *Green Line*, 47, p. 3 and 44, p. 4, and *Eco-News*, 35, p. 2.

12. *Eco-News*, 34, p. 3.

13. *Green Line*, May 1987, p. 4.

14. As for instance in *Labour's Charter for the Environment* (London, n.d.). For a Green Party view of how the other parties are responding to public concern on the environment, while – the Greens argue – failing to take the issue seriously, see the pamphlet *Green Politics: Fact and Fiction* (London, n.d.).

15. For the founding statement of the Association of Socialist Greens, see *Green Line*, February 1988, p. 4. The Association is specifically, and exclusively, for socialists who are members of the Green Party. Some Green Party members have previously been, and are still, members of SERA (Socialist Environment and Resources Association) also: I, for one, am a member of both.

16. Hilary Wainwright, *Labour: A Tale of Two Parties* (London 1987), p. 277.

17. See Jane Dibblin, *Day of Two Suns: US Nuclear Testing and the Pacific Islanders* (London 1988), on nuclear testing in the Pacific, including British tests in Australia. It is no exaggeration to say that this one book contains sufficient material, most of it unknown to the general public, to form the basis of a major campaign linking issues of self-determination, militarism and nuclear technology.

18. See chapter 2 above, especially the discussion of general and particular interests in the section on Class.

19. Quoted in Wainwright, *ibid.*, p. 301.

20. The precise effect would depend on how much the vote fell in particular constituencies: Labour in fact has many 'safe seats' in the north and in Scotland which it would retain even if its share of the vote fell sharply. But Richard Kuper points out, in his argument for PR in *Interlink* 2, p. 2, that at the 1983 general election the Alliance, which gained over 25 per cent of the popular vote, had fewer than 4 per cent of seats in the Commons.

21. Kuper, *art. cit.*

22. Wainwright, *ibid.*, p. 277.

23. *Green Line*, 53, p. 20. See his other articles on the same theme in *Green Line*, 58 and 59. On Green–Liberal contacts, see *Green Line*, 59, p. 3.

24. *Ibid.*

25. Kuper, *art. cit.*

26. Raymond Williams, 'Socialism and Ecology' (pamphlet), published by SERA (London n.d.), p. 20.

Index of authors mentioned and quoted in the text